DANGER IN THE DESERT
TRUE ADVENTURES OF
A DINOSAUR HUNTER

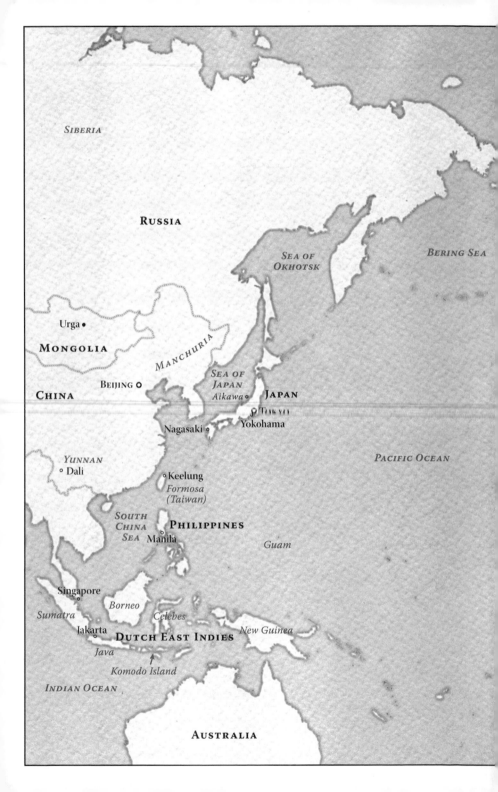

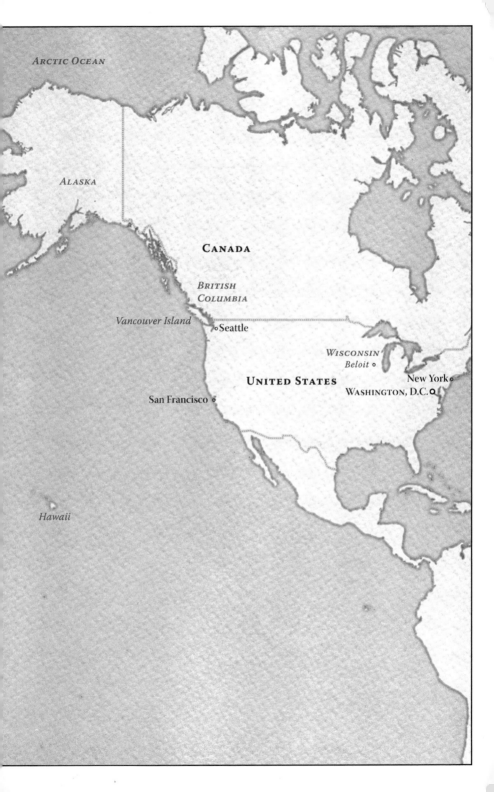

Roy Chapman Andrews

DANGER IN THE DESERT
TRUE ADVENTURES OF
A DINOSAUR HUNTER

ROGER COHEN

STERLING

New York / London
www.sterlingpublishing.com/kids

A FLYING POINT PRESS BOOK

It is our belief that any good story, whether fiction or non-fiction, requires dialog to give the reader a sense of immediacy. This is especially important when writing books for young people. It is equally important to be faithful to historical accuracy. We feel strongly that any dialog included in a book should be based on sources such as journals and autobiographies. In no case should dialog be included that in any way distorts the facts of the story. We strive to publish books that live up to these standards.

Design: John T. Perry III and PlutoMedia
Front cover photographs: American Museum of Natural History
(AMNH 241736, 410767)
Frontispiece photograph: American Museum of Natural History (AMNH 411083)
Interior photographs: American Museum of Natural History (AMNH 411042s, 410783, 258366,
24333, 2A25639, 228955, 410955, 410780, 410760)

Library of Congress Catalog-in-Publication Data

Cohen, Roger
Danger in the desert : true adventures of a dinosaur huter / Roger Cohen.
p. cm. — (Sterling point books)
Includes bibliographical references and index.
ISBN-13: 978-1-4027- 5706-8
ISBN-10: 1-4027- 5706-9
1. Andrews, Roy Chapman, 1884-1960—Juvenile literature. 2. Paleontologists—United
States—Biography—Juvenile literature. 3. Dinosaurs—Juvenile literature. 4. Voyages and
travels—Juvenile literature. I. Title.

QE707.A53C64 2008
560.92—dc22
2007051032
[B]

2   4   6   8   10   9   7   5   3   1

Published by Sterling Publishing Co., Inc.
387 Park Avenue South, New York, NY 10016
Copyright © 2008 by Roger Cohen
Maps copyright © 2008 by Richard Thompson, Creative Freelancers, Inc.
Charts and drawings copyright © 2008 by John T. Perry III
Distributed in Canada by Sterling Publishing
c/o Canadian Manda Group, 165 Dufferin Street
Toronto, Ontario, Canada M6K 3H6
Distributed in the United Kingdom by GMC Distribution Services
Castle Place, 166 High Street, Lewes, East Sussex, England BN7 IXU
Distributed in Australia by Capricorn Link (Australia) Pty. Ltd.
P.O. Box 704, Windsor, NSW 2756, Australia

Printed in China
All rights reserved

Sterling ISBN-13: 978-1-4027-5706-8
ISBN-10: 1-4027-5706-9

For information about custom editions, special sales, premium and
corporate purchases, please contact Sterling Special Sales
Department at 800-805-5489 or specialsales@sterlingpublishing.com.

For the Mongolian countryside:

One cannot divine nor forecast the conditions that will make happiness; one only stumbles upon them by chance, in a lucky hour, at the world's end somewhere, and holds fast to the days . . .
—Willa Cather

CONTENTS

CONTENTS

"THERE IT IS," MY FRIEND SAID. "CAN YOU see it? It's right below that small dune."

I looked out the dusty window of the slowly moving jeep and saw the *ger* in the distance. The squat, round dwelling, which Mongolians had resided in for over a thousand years, was surrounded by a flock of goats, sheep and two-humped camels. The animals pecked at the shrubs and small clumps of grass in the rocky earth while two young boys in T-shirts and baseball caps herded them toward the open plain.

I gazed out across the Gobi, one of the largest deserts in the world, when the jeep suddenly bounced into a pothole, jolting everyone from their seats and knocking our heads against the ceiling. I plopped down like a sack of potatoes and heard the driver chuckling to himself.

"Sorry about that, my friends. Unfortunately, we don't have paved roads in the Gobi! But, never mind—we're here!"

He stopped in front of the *ger,* and we opened the doors, parting the herd of animals trudging around either side of the jeep. An elderly man crouched through the short doorway of the *ger* and greeted us in his long *dell* robe. After adjusting the dark green sash around his waist, he extended his hand.

"This is my grandfather," my friend said. "He's wanted to meet my American friend for quite some time."

I shook his hand firmly. "Very nice to meet you," I said in Mongolian.

"How was your trip?" he asked, offering me a smoothly polished agate snuff bottle with his right hand.

"Excellent," I answered. I accepted the bottle and politely rubbed a tiny amount of the tobacco against my nostrils, as Mongolian custom dictated. "Your grandson tells me you used to be a geologist . . . at the university in the city."

"That's right. I just came back a few years ago to retire. I spent much of my career traveling through the Gobi and lecturing on the geology of the desert. In the last few years, I also brought my students to a few of the sites first discovered by Andrews."

"Andrews?"

"You haven't heard of him? I thought he would be famous in your country. Perhaps it was too long ago . . . Come with me. I'll show you."

My friend and the driver went inside while the old man led me up the short sand dune behind the *ger*. When we reached the top, he pointed to several low, rounded mountains on the southeastern horizon.

"You see those?" he said, pointing with his out-stretched finger. "Less than a day's drive beyond the mountains are some of the richest sites of dinosaur bones in the world. Many of them were found by a famous explorer from your country. His name was Andrews."

We heard the *ger* door open and the voice of a young girl. "Grandpa . . . the tea's ready."

"Ah yes, the tea. Let's go inside, my friend, and I'll tell you the rest of story . . ."

Roger Cohen
Gobi Desert
July 1998

I was born to be an explorer. There was never any decision to make. I couldn't do anything else and be happy. . . . The desire to see new places, to discover new facts—the curiosity of life has always been a resistless driving force in me.

—Roy Chapman Andrews

CHAPTER 1

LOST IN THE GOBI

South Gobi Desert, Mongolia

Summer 1922

"*BLAST!*"

Roy Chapman Andrews banged his fist on the steering wheel in rage. He had just rolled to a stop at the base of a large and twisting sand dune. Though he hated to admit it, he knew that his team was still lost. Hoping to glimpse a way out of the forbidding desert valley, he jumped out of the car and trudged up the sand, his knee-high leather boots sinking into the side of the hill. Halfway up the dune, Roy turned and scanned the horizon. He drummed his fingers on his holstered revolver, contemplating his next move. Through the intense glare of the sun he could make out only the same endless expanse that he had seen for the last two days. It was a harsh landscape of fine pebbles and sand, crumbled brown earth and stubby light green shrubs peeking out through jagged cracks in the ground.

Soon the other four Dodge convertibles pulled up, trailing immense clouds of dust in their wake. The members of the expedition left their cars and immediately headed toward the lee of the dune to take cover from the bright rays of the sun. Roy whistled for the head mechanic, Bayard Colgate, who was poking under the hood of the lead car, to join him on the dune.

"Find anything yet, Roy?" Bayard asked, after he had climbed up and handed his binoculars to the leader of the expedition.

Roy smiled through cracked lips at his apprentice. He had been impressed by his patience since they left Beijing earlier that summer; the young man had also displayed his talent at fixing anything that the desert could throw at their vehicles.

Roy took the binoculars and peered through them under the shade of his wide-brimmed fedora hat. He scanned the desert quietly for several minutes. Bayard stood stock still next to Roy and wondered how the man could remain so calm in a situation like this. When he was finished gazing across the desert, Roy slowly rubbed his dry lips with the back of his hand and turned back to Bayard.

"Well, I don't see any track, but I think I spotted a well," Roy said pointing east. "If we're lucky, some nomads will be along and point us in the right direction. Let's bring the cars around, and we'll camp there for the night. We'll see what we can find tomorrow."

Roy knew that although the desert might appear barren from a distance, on closer inspection it contained pockets of life every few miles. There were small wells or oases of green grass and trickling streams pinpricked across the terrain that had supported herders and animals for thousands of years. In fact a vast trading network of camel caravans that journeyed through this seemingly barren desert had flourished for centuries.

After looking through the binoculars once more, Roy was sure that the well he had seen was still in use. He hoped that a group of nomads might pass by to water their camels and direct the expedition to the route out of the desert. The team could then safely proceed to Northern China and their headquarters in Beijing.

Roy headed back to the car and signaled the men to move out. With Roy and Bayard in the lead, they spent the next hour bouncing over the bumpy terrain of the Gobi and arrived at the well before sunset. Sure enough, it was still functional and contained several feet of brackish water at the bottom of its deep pit. There were fresh camel tracks in the dirt leading away from the well, indicating it had most likely been used in the last forty-eight hours. With a renewed sense of optimism, the men quickly pitched their tents. As evening approached, they sat around a smoking fire of camel dung eating a supper of mutton jerky and biscuits.

When they were finished eating, Roy left the men to smoke their pipes under the stars. He and Walter Granger, the expedition's chief scientist, returned to Roy's tent to discuss their chances of making it out of the desert the next morning.

Two days earlier, the members of the expedition had decided to return as quickly as possible to Beijing since winter was fast approaching. Even though it was only August, the temperature in the Gobi was already dipping below freezing at night. They knew that winter in Mongolia brought arctic winds and temperatures plunging to –40 degrees Fahrenheit. So far, the expedition had been a tremendous success—the team had discovered new species of dinosaurs and obtained exceptional specimens of rare Gobi mammals for the American Museum of Natural History's collection and examined dozens of spectacular geologic formations. However, if they stayed longer with the onset of winter threatening, they could jeopardize their entire expedition.

The men agreed that returning by their original route would take too much time and that they should seek a shortcut through the Gobi. They would then hope to rendezvous with Merin, the head of their camel caravan, along the way. The camels carried gas for the cars as well as food and were essential for their expedition.

Their drive had started out well. Roy, Bayard, and the expedition's chief geologist, Charles Berkey, guided the cars by compass and map, and the party had made good progress toward a caravan trail that led the hundreds of miles back to Northern China.

But as Charles carefully surveyed their route, the three men realized that their earlier calculations were incorrect. The Russian maps that they had been using had been drawn decades earlier—and they had proved slightly inaccurate. The men were now lost, and they knew that in the unforgiving Gobi, another error could cost them their lives.

After realizing their mistake, Roy calmly gathered everyone together and told them the devastating news.

"We have water and supplies for maybe a week, ten days maximum," Andrews began, the scientists and Mongolian porters focused intently on him.

"We're going to follow the same route we're on. If we double back, we'll probably wind up getting even more lost than we are now. If we're lucky, we'll somehow find Merin and the camels. If not . . ." Roy paused, contemplating what would happen if they didn't locate the caravan and its supplies of gas and food. He knew that they would have to find a nomad encampment, and if they were lucky, purchase camels to ride out of the desert, a proposition that would put the expedition

Andrews scans the desert for trails.

months behind schedule. The men looked at Roy, knowing exactly what he had been thinking. After a few seconds, Walter Granger broke the silence.

"Well then, boys," he said in his fatherly manner, hoping to relax everyone's nerves in this tense situation, "I suppose we'd better be off." The men followed him to the cars and sped across the desert following Roy and Bayard. As they drove, the men looked intently for possible landmarks or trails that might guide them in the right direction. After hours of driving through the blistering heat and several crashes into potholes of sand that swallowed their front tires, they made it to the dune where Roy spotted the well. Now Roy and Walter were huddled together planning the next day's route.

The other men of the expedition, all leaders in their scientific fields and experienced travelers, sat outside finishing their pipes and drinking the last of the coffee, patiently waiting for Roy and Walter to emerge from the tent.

After a few minutes, the two joined their colleagues. "The best route," Roy began, looking into the eyes of the men he had hand picked months earlier to join him, "is to head due east. We might be able to push the cars and make it all the way back to Kalgan or another town in Northern China, but if we try that, there's too much of a risk that we'd run out of fuel. We've got to trust that Merin's made it through the desert and is waiting for us with those camels.

"Besides," Roy added, trying to bring some levity to their somewhat dire situation, "I'm not spending the entire winter in the Gobi knowing that our last bottle of bourbon is lying unopened in the bottom of Merin's saddlebag!"

The men chuckled, knowing that Roy meant it. They quickly agreed to the plan. Though most of the members of the expedition were world-famous scientists and were at least a decade his senior, they had come to respect and admire Roy like no one they had ever worked with. They knew that despite all the struggles it had taken to get their team through the Gobi, Roy had remained calm and projected a single-minded sense of vision. They also realized that he was risking his entire career on the success of the expedition, and if it failed, his reputation as an explorer would be shattered.

As the fire died down, the men bundled themselves in their sheepskin blankets against the freezing temperatures of the desert night. Regardless of the astounding scientific breakthroughs that they had made on the expedition, they knew that tomorrow would be the most important day of their months in the Gobi. If anything went wrong, they understood that not only their discoveries but also their lives might be in jeopardy.

CHAPTER 2

DISCOVERY OF THE FLAMING CLIFFS

South Gobi Desert, Mongolia

Summer 1922

THE EXPEDITION BROKE CAMP AND SET OUT at dawn. After only a few hours, a sandstorm slowly began drifting across their path, and they were soon driving through a cloud of fine yellow dust. When the fog of sand had become so thick that Roy could barely see the other vehicles, he tied the cars' bumpers front to back with short lengths of rope, and the caravan slowly continued east.

Finally, a little after noon, the wind picked up, taking with it the enormous clouds of dust. The men loosened the ropes and gunned the engines of the cars, trying to make up for lost time. Roy was concerned that they might have passed the track during the sandstorm but decided to press on.

As the afternoon sun reached its pinnacle and began to descend on its long, slow arc to meet the floor of the Gobi, the men became more worried. They were losing precious time.

Another hour passed, and the cars arrived at a gently sloping plateau leading up the side of the valley. As they drove up, hoping to get a wider view of the desert, Roy noticed a small brown speck on the horizon. He immediately braked the car and asked for the binoculars.

He took a brief look at what he had just seen.

"Thank God," he murmured below his breath as he lowered the binoculars. "We just might make it out of here."

Roy hurried into action. "Bayard, you wait here with the cars to see if they need any work. Tell Damdin to

12

come up and ride with me. I'm going to ask directions at that *ger* up there."

Damdin, the expedition's translator, ambled up to Roy's car wearing the typical *dell* robe and curved-toe riding boots worn by all Mongolian herders. He climbed into the passenger's seat of the Dodge and they drove toward the light brown *ger* half a mile to the north. As soon as Roy and Damdin pulled within a hundred yards of the large circular dwelling, two massive mangy dogs lying in the shade leapt to their feet. They growled, baring their sharp yellow teeth, and charged directly at the car.

Roy deftly grabbed the shovel that he kept in the backseat for this very occasion and stood up in the car, ready to beat back the vicious dogs. After spending the last several months in Mongolia, Roy had learned that each *ger* was protected by at least one enormous hound that could easily rip off a man's limb in less than a minute.

"Nohoi hoe, nohoi hoe!" Roy shouted. The two words, which meant "hold the dog," was the first and without

a doubt the most important Mongolian phrase he had ever learned.

Roy's request went unheeded, and seconds later, the two dogs were within feet of the vehicle, their forelegs extended and teeth bared, ready to strike. Just as one of the dogs seemed poised to lunge into the vehicle, the waist-high front door of the *ger* opened. An old man with white whiskers descending from his chin bent through the opening and peered curiously at the scene unfolding in front of his home. He walked toward the car and cursed at the dogs in a guttural burst of Mongolian.

Holding the shovel above his head, Roy was amazed to see the two dogs immediately back down and slink away to the back of the *ger*. The old man gestured for Roy and Merin to follow him inside, and they jumped out of the car and ducked into the *ger*.

As his eyes adjusted from being out of the blinding desert sun, Roy was confronted by the pungent odors inside the *ger*—old leather, boiled mutton, and the sharp tang of freshly churned butter. After a few seconds, Roy grew accustomed to the light and saw the old man sitting on a tiny stool behind a small fire in the center of the *ger*. On the rough carpet next to him were two small boys in stained *dells* playing what looked to be a game of marbles with small animal bones. The old man waved them over to two small stools beside him.

"*Sainbain uu,*" Roy said in as friendly a manner as possible. After the old man replied hello, Roy switched to Chinese, which Damdin spoke fluently, and began

Merin leads the camels in search of water.

asking the old man directions as his Mongolian assistant translated.

While the old man patiently listened to Damdin, he reached above the sash tied around his waist into the large opening at the front of his *dell*. He drew out a long-stemmed pipe and packed it with tobacco from a greasy cotton pouch. When Damdin had finished telling the old man how they had become lost and that they were looking for the route back to China, the aged herder grinned, showing his few remaining teeth loosely balanced on his dark red gums.

"Yes, yes, you're looking for the road," the old man replied, slowly nodding his head. "Many travelers are easily lost in this part of the desert. But, there's no worry. The road is only a few hours ride from here. First we'll have tea, and then I'll show you the way."

The old man thrust a twig into the coals of the fire and lifted the flame to the bowl of his pipe. He inhaled deeply, and the room filled with blue acrid smoke.

Just then a young woman wearing a blue silk *dell* walked into the *ger* and silently began making tea. Roy watched as she carefully set a large iron pot on the metal prongs above the hot coals. She then filled it with water ladled from a large wooden barrel by the front door. The woman scraped in flakes from a firmly pressed block of green tea and sprinkled in small chunks of rock salt. When the tea began to boil, she poured in a jar of milk and, after a few minutes, scooped the steaming concoction into a large wooden pitcher. Each person was served a bowl of the milk tea with a small pat of freshly made butter floating on top.

"Bayarthla." Roy thanked her. He sipped the tea and found it surprisingly refreshing. The woman placed a small bowl of what appeared to Roy as chunks of brownish-white brick on another stool in front of him.

"Aarul," the woman said.

"This is hardened milk curd," Damdin explained to Roy. "It's made in the pot right there and then hardened in the sun on the roof of the *ger*. We eat it almost every day."

Roy took a piece and looked around the *ger* while Damdin spoke to the old man. From what he

17

remembered on his first trip to Mongolia several years earlier, this comfortable living space was the ideal nomadic dwelling. It could be taken down in less than thirty minutes and the two wooden poles that supported the roof and the thick felt that covered the outside could be packed onto the back of a camel or horse in an instant. It could then be completely reestablished in no more than an hour. Roy marveled at its convenience.

Andrews was jolted from his thoughts when Damdin turned to him excitedly.

"He's just seen Merin and our caravan! He said the camels went through here only a few days ago! They're likely taking on water at Sair Us—an old caravan stop close to here. He said that the trail back to China runs right past it."

Roy couldn't believe his luck. Only hours ago, he thought that he had led the entire expedition into failure—and even possible death. He gulped down the rest of his tea and thanked the herders, leaving them a small box of safety matches—a highly prized gift for any family in the Gobi. He knelt down to say good-bye to the two children playing bone marbles. The younger boy took Roy by the hand and showed him how to flick the anklebone across the carpet. Just as Roy was taking aim, he heard a distant cry carry over the plateau and through the walls of the *ger*. He and Damdin looked at each other and jumped to their feet. Roy grabbed his hat, and the men bolted out of the *ger* figuring there was trouble.

Back in the sunlight, Roy squinted into the distance. He could barely make out Charles Berkey leaning over the front door of his car and repeatedly honking the horn trying to attract their attention. Roy and Damdin sprinted toward the cars and arrived out of breath to find that Charles had suddenly disappeared. Fearing that bandits had ambushed the cars, Roy drew his pistol. When he heard footsteps from behind, he grabbed Damdin by the sleeve and the two dove for cover behind Charles' car. Roy cocked the hammer of his revolver, and then inched his way up until he could peer over the hood.

Instead of the bandits that he had suspected, Roy saw Charles appear from a thin crack in the plateau just a few hundred yards away. To his surprise, he saw that his friend, one of the most venerable geologists in the world, looked more excited than a schoolboy.

Charles ran toward Roy with his arms open to the heavens. "We've done it!" he cried, jogging around the hood of the dusty car. He reached out to embrace Roy and Damdin in a bear hug.

"Roy, you're not going to believe this! We've found something big. I think it's something that no one's going to believe!"

Charles was too ecstatic to explain anything more. Instead, the men dashed after him to the long crack in the plateau less than a quarter of a mile away. As they arrived at the edge, Roy stood dumbfounded. Directly below him was a beautiful, gently sloping canyon with hourglass-shaped sandstone pillars and giant boulders crisscrossing the reddish-brown slope. It was unlike anything he had ever seen in the Gobi.

Roy spotted the rest of the team off to the right just below the edge of the canyon. They were on hands and knees peering intently at a small bump on the side of the slope. Charles eagerly handed over the binoculars and

Roy squinted through the lenses in disbelief. He watched as the scientists slowly brushed off the dust from a pale white dinosaur bone that seemed to be almost seven feet long and fully exposed to the sun. Roy now understood Berkey's excitement. He slowly lowered the binoculars and saw that his friend's grin was a mile-wide.

"It's the biggest we've seen all summer, Roy. We're still not sure what species it belongs to, but Walter has some ideas. But, that's not all, Roy. There are more . . . many more." Berkey then pointed downward and Roy saw that

Children in front of nomadic home or ger.

21

white dinosaur bones pockmarked the entire slope—
some were even exposed so greatly that they were ready
to be extracted with less than a few minutes digging. Roy
knew that they had stumbled across a fossil collector's
paradise that any paleontologist would have spent his
entire career seeking. Seized by the excitement of the
discovery, he followed Charles down the canyon for
a closer look while he listened to the story of how
Shackelford, the expedition's photographer, had located
this amazing find completely by accident.

"While you and Damdin were at the *ger,*" Charles
recounted as he stumbled over the loose rocks, careful to
avoid stepping on any bones that might be lying just
below the surface, "we waited in the vehicles playing
cards. Shackelford was getting bored and got out to
wander. He started looking for anything to photograph
and after only a couple minutes of poking around looking
through the camera, he almost fell down the canyon here
when he wasn't paying attention."

Indeed, when Roy first approached the top of the
canyon, it had appeared to be only a thin crack in the

plateau. If he hadn't been standing directly on top of it, Roy would never even have noticed the significant discoveries that lay directly beneath him.

Stumbling down the hill with Charles, Roy was amazed at the wealth of fossils surrounding him. There were perfectly intact oval-shaped skulls with rows of sharp teeth jutting out of the eroded sandstone, long pale-white leg bones, and even what looked to be an entire dinosaur skeleton covered by less than an inch of sand. Looking around him, Roy knew that no matter how much of a hurry they were in to beat the winter and make it back to China, they had to camp here, at least for a day.

The team spent the rest of the day combing the hillside and marking the position of each fossil, so they could carry them out of the desert by their camel caravan when they returned next summer. After hours of feverish work, the men gathered at the top of the canyon for supper and to revel in their amazing stroke of luck. As their conversation echoed down the canyon, the sun finally began to set across the open desert. When the deep yellow orb settled on the horizon, the men were awestruck as the last beams of sun made the hill below them glow an intense fiery red, reflecting brilliant shadows from the rocks and flat-topped mesas at the base of the canyon. The men sat silently as they gazed at the view until darkness slowly fell. That night, the men named the area the Flaming Cliffs, a name that would soon be on the tongue of every scientist and explorer around the world.

Later that evening, Roy whispered the name under his breath while he sat in his chair on the rim of the canyon. Today had been without a doubt the high point of his career. He knew that the discoveries they had made at the Flaming Cliffs would prove to the world that the enormous gamble of leading an expensive expedition into the heart of one of the world's last unexplored regions was worth every penny. Most important, he knew that his mentor, Henry Fairfield Osborn, the venerable president of the American Museum of Natural History, would be ecstatic once he heard the news of what they had found today.

Thinking of him, Roy smiled as he recalled how he had first met Osborn after he had arrived in New York City, a green kid right out of college ready to travel the world. But his lust for adventure hadn't started when he arrived at the museum. Roy reminisced, as he often did when he was alone at the end of a hard day of traveling in the Gobi, that the seeds for his future life of exploration had been planted long ago during his boyhood in Wisconsin.

CHAPTER 3

YOUNG EXPLORER

Beloit, Wisconsin

1890s

FOR AS LONG AS HE COULD REMEMBER, ROY knew that he wanted to be an explorer. Whenever he recalled his childhood, there never seemed to be a time when he wasn't tramping through the woods near his small hometown, hunting or fishing with friends, or reading *Robinson Crusoe* by the fire. These early experiences had taught him how to survive in the outdoors and fostered the independent spirit that would later sustain him on his many adventures across the globe.

From a young age, Roy also learned the importance that luck would play throughout his life. The first time he realized this was when he narrowly escaped trouble after his ninth birthday. He had received his first shotgun as a gift from his father and the next day at dawn, Roy filled his canteen, packed a sandwich, stuffed his jacket pockets with ammunition, and headed into the woods for his first hunting excursion alone.

For the entire day, he trudged through the brush taking aim at squirrels and ducks but never getting close enough for a clean shot. He walked for miles stalking prey, and as the sun began to set, he was exhausted and decided to turn for home. Returning on a different trail though a large grove of trees, he spotted a pond surrounded by thick rushes with a small flock of geese drifting gently toward the bank. Roy knew that this was the chance he had been waiting for all day. He quietly reloaded his shotgun and crept toward the water.

Roy squatted next to a bush at the water's edge and watched the geese move slowly across the far side of the pond. As he lifted his gun, Roy knew that he'd be returning home that night with supper for his mother. He then carefully steadied the wooden stock against his shoulder like his father had taught him and took aim. He looked down the sight, exhaled slowly, and then squeezed the trigger. The shotgun responded with a thunderous boom and jerked upward in his hands. Roy gripped the gun tightly and waited in the thick brush while the powder smoke cleared. He looked across the pond and saw that the geese hadn't budged. They instead appeared to be slowly sinking into the water.

A second later he saw a man in an orange hunting cap leap to his feet on the bank only a few yards from the geese.

"What in the blazes is going on here?" he yelled, his beet red face flashing a look of pure anger. The man jumped into the pond and waded up to his knees, looking back and forth hoping to catch whoever had fired the gun.

Roy had ducked into the brush as soon as he saw the man emerge across the pond. He watched as the man slowly crept through the water trying to keep his balance on the muddy bottom. A few seconds later, he reached the ducks and picked them up in his hands. Roy then realized what he had done. The geese he had shot weren't geese at all. They were inflatable hunting decoys!

Roy saw the man's head turn in his direction. From twenty yards away, he could see the man's furrowed brow and lips pulled back in rage.

"Come out, blast you! Do you have any idea how much these decoys cost!"

The man then began to trudge toward him through the water. Roy's blood froze. He had no idea what the man might do if he caught him. His parents would certainly give him a hiding and take away his gun after he'd had it only a day. As the man drew closer, Roy knew that he had no other choice. Without a second thought, he jumped to his feet, turned on his heels and ran. Though his house was more than two miles away, he didn't stop once. By the time he raced down the sidewalk and through his front door, his cheeks were bright pink and his cap was soaked with sweat despite the winter cold.

Roy ran into his room and slammed the door. He

snatched off his hat and threw it on the dresser. He began stripping off his jacket—when he stopped cold. The man's face flashed through his mind, and Roy remembered that he had seen him before. In the few seconds after he had shot the decoys at the pond, he had been too frightened by the man to recognize who he was. Roy now realized that it was his father's acquaintance, Fred. In a small town like Beloit, Roy knew that his father would eventually find out what had happened. If he discovered that his son had deliberately withheld the truth, well, Roy couldn't even bear to think of what his father might do. He knew that this time, he wouldn't be getting out of trouble. He finished taking off his jacket, opened his bedroom door, and walked to the kitchen where his parents were fixing dinner.

Roy crept into a chair and sat across from his parents who were busy snapping beans at the table.

"Oh, I'm glad you're back," his mother said. "We could use a hand."

Roy took a bean and stared at it in his lap, picking at the green skin with his index finger.

"Are you all right Roy? Anything wrong?" his father asked.

Roy looked up. He then opened his mouth and before he even knew what was happening, the entire story was spilling out. When he had finished, he threw the bean back onto the table and stood up. He squinted his eyes shut, bracing himself for his father to start hollering at him. But, the only sound he heard was his father clearing his throat and then laughing uproariously.

"You mean you *shot* Fred's decoys?" his father said, still chuckling to himself. "Oh, Roy, that's perfect! It's about time Fred loosens up a little. He spends his entire day playing with those darn things like they were his own kids! I can't wait to tell the boys at the barbershop about this! Roy, you done good. I'm going to get you a better gun, so you can blow away his decoys any time you like!"

Roy couldn't believe his ears. By pure chance he had gotten out of a jam. Every time he went duck hunting over the next few years, he remembered that his father had been true to his word. His top of the line double-barreled shotgun was the envy of every other boy in town.

CHAPTER 4

NEARLY DROWNED

AS A TEENAGER, ROY BECAME AN EVEN MORE avid outdoorsman and learned many of the valuable skills that he'd use later in his career as an explorer. He taught himself how to navigate by the stars, make animal traps with objects he could find in the wilderness, and track wild game by carefully examining fresh trail prints and scat. He also began collecting Indian arrowheads and plants that he found on the outskirts of Beloit, which he mounted and framed on his bedroom wall. As he became more of an expert in the backcountry during his adolescence, he began taking up a hobby that would not only become his passion but also end up putting him through college.

During Roy's youth, the practice of taxidermy, or mounting animals for display in their original skin, was rapidly changing. Up until then, if a hunter wished to display his trophy, he usually took it to have the animal's skin stuffed with cotton or old rags. This was easy to accomplish but resulted in the mount looking painfully artificial. When new methods and materials became available, however, the craft of taxidermy began to evolve and change into a genuine art form. Taxidermists were now able to experiment with new tanning techniques to make the animal's skin look much more life-like. They also began encasing the animal's bones in plaster and mounting them in anatomically correct poses. Taxidermists now could also more effectively recreate an animal's eyes, nose, and teeth, so they seemed genuine to the touch.

As Roy began to read of these developments in books he checked out from the library, he realized that by studying this new field, he could learn anatomy, skin tanning, sculpting, and dissecting—all skills he knew were important for any budding naturalist.

Roy soon began practicing taxidermy with his own hunting trophies whenever he had a free moment, and by the time he was in high school, he had progressed so quickly that he was regarded as one of Beloit's experts. During hunting season, Roy's skills were in such high demand that by the time he was a senior ready to graduate, he had easily made enough money to cover his college tuition.

Roy decided to stay close to home for the next four years to study at Beloit College and continue his explorations of rural Wisconsin. By his own admission, Roy was never an outstanding student, though he of course continued to immerse himself in the study of natural history. His love for the outdoors continued unabated throughout college and with his English instructor, Monty White, he explored the woods and swamps around Beloit extensively.

One crisp spring day, Monty and Roy decided to head to the woods for some light hunting and canoeing. As they paddled deeper down the river into the forest, Roy began to hear the distinct quacking of ducks just around the bend. He dug his paddle deeper into the water and eyed the same shotgun that his father had purchased for him more than ten years ago. Monty was eager to bag his share of ducks too and began paddling quickly to keep up with Roy. Just as they were about to turn toward the ducks, Monty lost his grip on the paddle, and it slipped out of his hand into the river.

"Hold on a sec, Roy," Monty said, gesturing for Roy to stop paddling. "Let me grab the paddle, and we'll be on those ducks in no time!"

Roy watched as Monty leaned out of the canoe to reach for the paddle. His fingertips brushed the wooden shaft, but it was just out of reach. Roy tried to steer the canoe closer, but before he could get his paddle into the water, Monty rose into a crouch and lunged for the loose paddle. The canoe instantly tipped dangerously to the left, and Roy grabbed for the right gunwale to steady the boat. It was too late, though. He heard Monty splash into the river and an instant later, the canoe capsized over Roy's head sending him plunging under the icy water.

A swift current began carrying Roy downriver, and he became frantic as he tried to fight his way to the surface against the undertow. Roy struggled underwater for almost a minute, his arms and legs pounding and his chest ready to explode. He knew that he would die if he didn't get out of the water immediately. With his last ounce of energy, he kicked his legs and tried swimming toward the bank. A few seconds later, his hand brushed against the mud of the shore. He grabbed a clump of reeds and pulled himself to the surface. Gasping for breath he crawled through the mud until he was sprawled on the bank. He lifted his head, spat out a stream of green river water, and collapsed back onto the ground. Roy lay there in shock, amazed that he had survived.

Roy lacked the strength to stand but knew from his long experience in the outdoors that if he and Monty didn't find help immediately, they'd most likely develop hypothermia and perhaps die next to the river. He commanded himself to stand up and see where his friend had made it out of the river. Gathering all of his remaining strength, he took a quick breath of air, and pulled himself up until he was on all fours looking down the bank.

"Monnnnntyyyyyy!" Roy screamed with all the energy he could muster. His voice echoed without an answer across the marsh. Roy had seen Monty plunge into the water after the canoe tipped over but hadn't been worried. Monty was an excellent swimmer, and he had fallen into the water only yards from the bank. In the meantime, Roy had almost died trying to save his own life and had no time to think of what had happened to his friend.

Roy called for Monty a second time. When he heard only the sound of the water cascading over the rocks, he stood up and looked across the river. There was no sign of Monty anywhere. Roy hobbled up and down the bank for the next ten minutes positive that he would spot his friend comfortably relaxing on shore. This had to be a joke! Surely he would have heard me by now, he thought. As Roy continued searching, he looked carefully through the brush expecting to find Monty hiding with a smile on his face over the pickle he had gotten them into.

After another thirty minutes of combing the riverbank for his friend, it began to turn dark, and Roy knew that this was no longer a joke. He knew deep down what had happened to Monty, but couldn't accept the fact that he wasn't going to find his friend. When Roy started shivering, he knew that if he didn't give up searching now, he wouldn't make it out alive.

Roy began to stumble through the woods. The heavy spring rains had inundated the ground, turning it into a thick stew of mud, broken twigs, and rocks. Roy had lost his shoes in the river and his bare feet squelched through the sludge. He slipped every few minutes, twisting his ankles and falling into the muck. Despite the pain and cold, Roy prodded himself to keep moving, and after almost an hour, he came to another river trickling through a clearing in the woods.

There was no way around the river. After surveying

the water carefully in the moonlight, he saw the shadow of a large flat stone just underneath the current. It was only a few feet between each bank of the river, and Roy knew he could leap across easily. He jumped to the rock, and when he landed, a jolt of pain shot through his swollen ankle. He slipped backward and tumbled into the water for the second time. As he sank to the bottom, Roy knew that he had wasted his last chance, and he lacked the energy to keep fighting. He drifted down through the water and despite the frigid temperature, a warm sensation came over him. He felt that he could go to sleep forever.

As he hit the bottom of the stream, Roy winced in pain again. He reached for his leg and felt a jagged wound on his calf that spewed blood into the river. He then tried to move, but he had fallen on an old strip of barbed wire stuck to the bottom and had entangled his clothes on its sharp stakes. The warm blood continued to spill out of his leg while he desperately yanked on the wire, trying to break free.

The pain had given him a renewed sense of vigor, and with a sharp tug, he tore his pants off the wire and quickly swam to the surface. He pulled himself out of the water and sat panting for breath beside the stream. The gash on his leg was gaping wide, but he couldn't give up now. If he only focused his mind and relied on his skills as an outdoorsman, he knew he could find his way home.

Roy stood up, oriented himself by the North Star, and began staggering westward back to town, blood still trickling down his leg. After only a few minutes, the forest cleared, and Roy found himself on the edge of a small wheat field. He spotted a house where a man in a rocking chair was smoking a pipe on the front porch. When the farmer saw Roy in his disheveled state, he leaped from his chair to help him. It was Roy's last sight before he collapsed onto the ground and blacked out.

For an entire day Roy slept. He dreamed about Monty falling into the water and watched helplessly as his friend sank beneath the surface. An instant later he felt himself being pulled under as he fell out of the canoe. Roy tossed in his bed while he remembered every moment that he spent struggling for his life in the freezing water.

Roy woke up with a start, his bed sheets drenched in sweat. His parents and the family doctor hurried to his bedside, glad that he was finally conscious. Still in shock from his nightmare, Roy had trouble grasping where he was.

"This is the Henderson's, Roy," his father began, leaning over the bed to stroke his son's forehead.

"You've been asleep almost eighteen hours. Mr. Henderson brought you in last night when he spotted you in the field. You were almost frozen solid!"

Roy looked at his father. He was still too disoriented to comprehend what had happened to him. Tears began to well up in his eyes as he thought of his friend. He struggled to ask if they had found anything—he formed the words in his mind but found that he was unable to speak. His father leaned closer.

"Monty . . ." was the only word that Roy was able to whisper.

After seeing the look in his father's eyes, Roy knew the

41

answer to his question. He fell back into his pillow and closed his eyes, still too exhausted and upset to mourn over Monty's death.

"I think we'd better give Roy some time to himself," the doctor said. His parents slowly followed the doctor out of the bedroom, leaving Roy alone once more. He lay on the bed in disbelief at what had happened the day before. He couldn't understand how he had survived while Monty, a champion swimmer who had fallen in the water so close to the bank, had drowned almost instantly. Roy knew he was lucky to be alive, and while he drifted off to sleep, he promised himself that he would spend the rest of his life taking nothing for granted. He would also work twice as hard to keep luck in his corner.

CHAPTER 5

NEW YORK CITY

IT TOOK MONTHS FOR ROY TO RECOVER FROM Monty's death. The experience had weighed so heavily on him that he began to lose his hair and spent much of his time sitting by himself on his parents' back porch. As his graduation from college approached, however, Roy slowly got better, and his thoughts turned to his future. He wanted to be an explorer and continue his outdoor adventures but still didn't have a concrete plan on how to pursue his dream.

When a zoologist from the American Museum of Natural History spoke at the school, Roy knew that he had found his calling. He had already read dozens of articles about how the museum had spearheaded scientific research and exploration for the last several decades. As the scientist described his latest projects, Roy became convinced that his destiny lay with the museum.

Immediately after the lecture, Roy returned to his room and typed a letter to Hermon Carey Bumpus, the museum's director, inquiring if there were any positions available for an eager college graduate. A few weeks later, Roy received a response telling him that there were no jobs available but that he was free to visit the museum if he was ever in Manhattan. Undeterred by the news, Roy packed his trunk, bought a train ticket, and waited for the last few weeks of the semester to finish. The day after graduation, he rose at dawn and boarded the overnighter to New York City.

Two days later, Roy stepped off a cross-town bus and walked down the street until he arrived at the imposing stone columns of the museum. He was so nervous that he couldn't lift his twitching legs up the stairs to the main entrance. For the next ten minutes, Roy stood on the street watching the traffic rush by and trying to find the courage to enter the museum. He was still in shock from saying good-bye to his parents on the quiet train platform in Beloit only a few days earlier. When he had calmed himself down, Roy took a deep breath and slowly marched up the stairs.

He walked into the museum's enormous foyer, his brand new wingtips tapping loudly against the checkered marble floor. As he approached the receptionist, Roy tried to look as professional as possible in the new suit that hung on his gangly six-foot frame.

"I'm here to see the director," Roy croaked nervously in a low-pitched voice.

The prim receptionist lowered her glasses and eyed Roy quizzically. "And, do you have an appointment, young man?"

Roy froze, not quite prepared for the question. He then fumbled in his jacket pocket for the letter he had received several weeks earlier and handed it to the woman.

"I don't have a fixed appointment, no ma'am," Roy began, "but as you can see, I have a personal invitation. So, I'm sure the director could spare a minute . . ."

The receptionist picked up the phone and spoke in a hushed tone. Roy looked back and forth in awe at the massive room in which he now stood.

"The director is in a meeting now, but if you'll wait over there, he'll be with you shortly," the receptionist said, pointing toward a wooden bench set against the wall.

Roy took a seat on the edge of the bench, barely able to contain his excitement. He watched men pass by in lab coats and three-piece suits and imagined himself striding next to them immersed in scientific discussions. As he continued to wait, he turned his eye from the clock to the receptionist every few seconds, ready to jump to his feet the moment she gestured him inside.

After sitting more than an hour, his stomach began to growl. It was now nearing lunch, and Roy was beginning to wonder if he had been too confident when he left Beloit. "Why would the head of one of the world's

greatest museums talk to someone like me?" he thought
to himself.

He looked at the clock again and suddenly out of the
corner of his eye saw the receptionist waving at him. Roy
stood up and nearly fell back against the wall. His legs
had fallen asleep while he had waited on the hard bench,
and after shaking them out, he stumbled over to the
receptionist's desk.

"Mr. Bumpus will see you now," the receptionist said,
eyeing Roy carefully.

She led Roy up the stairs and through the halls of the
museum's various display galleries on animals, prehistoric peoples, the cosmos, and oceanic life. They
walked down a narrow corridor and, at the very end, the
receptionist stopped at a door with a window of frosted
glass. She opened it swiftly and stood back, allowing Roy
to enter.

"Please take a seat in the director's office. He'll be with
you shortly."

Roy stepped into the huge office while the receptionist
closed the door behind him. Its walls were covered with

bookcases filled with dusty scientific tomes and old survey maps hanging on the walls. Roy pulled up a chair across from the director's massive wooden desk. Just as he sat down, the director strode into his office from a side door. Roy jumped to his feet.

"Sit, sit," Mr. Bumpus commanded. He then eased into his tall leather chair, laced his fingers together on his desk, and eyed Roy over his thin gold-rimmed spectacles.

"So, you got my letter. I'm afraid, son, that we still don't really have any openings here. Have you checked the other museums in town?" The director looked at Roy matter-of-factly across his desk. He was impressed with the young man's persistence, but over the years he had heard from many new graduates just like him asking for jobs.

Roy stammered, unsure of how to respond. He began telling the director all of the skills that he had learned in school and how he might be of use to the museum. But Roy saw that the director's attention was waning and stopped in mid-sentence. He decided to change tactics.

"Sir, I'll be honest with you. I'll do anything to work here—anything! Well . . . I'll even mop the floors!"

The director laughed, "Now why would a college boy like you want to mop floors?"

"Sir, these aren't just floors. These are the floors of the greatest natural history museum in the world, and it would be an honor to clean them!"

The director was impressed with Roy's answer. He also saw something special in Roy's eyes that he had never seen in the scores of young men that had sat across his desk. He then made a snap decision that would change Roy's life forever.

"Well, Mr. Andrews, you may be in luck. Jimmy Clark might need an assistant in the taxidermy department. You can start right away. But, I'm not going to forget what you said. For the first three months that you're here, I want the floors spotless before you head home every night."

CHAPTER 6

THE BEACHED WHALE

OVER THE NEXT SEVERAL MONTHS ROY LEARNED all the latest developments in taxidermy and rubbed shoulders with many of the world famous scientists working at the museum. He became fast friends with his new boss, Jimmy Clark, as they worked on the construction of a life-size whale model. In order to create the most realistic model possible, the two men did extensive research on *cetology,* the study of water mammals such as whales, dolphins, and porpoises.

One day the museum received word that a whale had washed up on a Long Island beach less than fifty miles outside of the city. Naturally, the director assigned Roy and Jimmy the task of retrieving the skeleton.

"This is of the utmost importance, gentlemen," they remembered the director saying. "I want photos, measurements, each and every bone, the baleen—everything! Now go get us the whale!" Roy walked out of the director's office with Jimmy, knowing that this was the opportunity he had been waiting for.

Before he began studying whales at the museum, Roy hadn't been much interested in the subject. As his investigations increased, he realized how little was known about the world's largest mammals and quickly became captivated by these giants of the ocean. He discovered that despite the tremendous importance of whaling to the world's economy in the previous century, almost no one had bothered to collect skeletons or study the mammals in the wild.

Roy saw an opportunity with his trip to Long Island. It might provide him with his first real scientific discovery and just as importantly would help him get noticed as a genuine member of the museum's staff.

It was bitter cold when Roy and Jimmy found the whale carcass half submerged in the white surf. The two men waded into the freezing water, tied the whale to a nearby rock, and took dozens of photographs and measurements. When they were finished, they began carving away huge chunks of blubber and flesh in order to retrieve the skeleton. At the end of the day, they were tired, soaking wet, and nowhere near finished.

The next morning, Roy and Jimmy returned to find the whale still lolling in the surf. They knew it was impossible to complete the work themselves, so instead hired several fishermen to assist them. In another two days of excruciating work of cutting the flesh and even boiling down the blubber to retrieve some of the smaller bones, they had finally completed the job. Roy and Jimmy were exhausted, but they had retrieved the museum's first complete whale skeleton. Upon their return to the museum, they were congratulated by the director and received the honor of preparing the bones for display.

Over the next several months, Roy became the museum's authority on cetaceans. He often worked late into the night studying whatever he could on the subject in the museum's library and dissecting organs of whales that he had collected himself. Roy believed, though, that if his superiors truly desired to have a first-class exhibit on the subject to educate the museum's growing number of visitors, he would have to study whales in the field first hand. After Roy had read a newspaper article on the whaling industry in Vancouver Island, he hatched a plan to propose to the director.

Several days later, Roy found himself back in Dr. Bumpus' office, perched on the edge of his chair opposite the desk. "You see, sir," Roy began, nervously outlining his proposal to the museum's preoccupied director. "Whaling is still commonly practiced in the Pacific Northwest. If I were to go out there, it would be a perfect opportunity to study whales in their natural habitat over an extended period—something that no other scientist has ever really done. It's a simple idea, but no one has ever tried it."

When Roy finished talking, Dr. Bumpus questioned him for over an hour on the details of the trip. He had never allowed such a young employee to plan an expedition on the museum's budget, but he couldn't forget the outstanding job Roy had done with the whale on Long Island. He looked across his desk once more and decided to take a risk.

"Okay, Andrews, we'll grant you a thousand dollars and three months leave. Come back with as much information as you can, and hopefully your findings will prove to be useful." Without another word, the director lowered his head and went back to work.

Roy couldn't believe his ears. He was so overwhelmed that he barely squeaked out a thank you to the director as he stood up and walked out of the room. He smiled as he strode down the halls of the museum that he had mopped only weeks earlier. He had achieved his dream and could now boast to anyone that he was a genuine professional explorer.

Roy spent the next few weeks perfecting his skills in the new art of photography and purchasing the provisions he'd need for the trip. Finally after a long cross-country train ride, he arrived at one of Canada's largest whaling stations on Vancouver Island, British Columbia. After stepping off the boat, he followed the director of the station down the pier and into the main building. As soon as he walked through the door, he nearly vomited from the overpowering stench. Huge chunks of humpback and blue whale carcasses littered the floor. Workers in blood-drenched aprons were feverishly cutting off the valuable blubber from the whales with long hacksaws and discarding the organs in gigantic heaps at their feet.

When Roy recovered from the shock of the disgusting smell, he dropped his bag and began clicking away with his camera. The busy workmen stopped to stare. The gore covering the warehouse floor was something that had never held the interest of anyone before. To the men, the large beasts splayed before them were for profit only. The blubber would be turned into heating oil and the flexible baleen fibers used for clothing. To Roy, they were a scientific gold mine that, if properly studied, could yield many new discoveries.

The next day, Roy went whale hunting for the first

time with a captain of a hundred-foot steamer. Most people believed that whales were gentle creatures, but Roy knew that when they were threatened, their enormous power was something that could kill an entire crew within minutes. Roy attempted to put this thought out of his mind as he stood beside the captain on the bridge of the ship.

After they had been at sea for only an hour, the captain caught sight of a whale breaking the surface of the white-capped waves. Roy was amazed as the whale powerfully cruised through the water, raising its huge tail flukes out of the ocean and diving rapidly below.

The captain pushed the throttle forward and followed the direction of the whale. About twenty minutes later, Roy viewed the huge mass of the humpback appear out of the depths of the water on the starboard side of the boat.

"There she blows!" the captain yelled.

One of the crew had already positioned himself on the deck and was taking aim with the harpoon. He waited until the whale was just about to break the surface, and then squeezed the trigger. The harpoon sailed through the air and punctured the side of the whale with a loud pop. Immediately after impact, the whale raised its hulking body into the air and landed with a massive splash that covered the sides of the boat in white spray.

The whale dove underwater, taking with it the thick metal chain attached to the harpoon. Roy watched as the wooden roller of chain nailed to the deck spun into a blur as the great beast tugged it deeper into the ocean. The captain cut the engines and let the whale drag the boat. After almost half an hour, they slowly came to a stop, and Roy watched as the whale came floating to the surface. Roy was an experienced hunter, but the sight of the beautiful animal floating dead in the water gave him pause. He turned to the captain and asked if it was ever difficult taking the lives of these animals every day.

"Aye, lad, they're remarkable beasts. But, this whale here will bring thousands of dollars, and I've got a boat to keep and a family to feed." Roy nodded his head silently as the captain began steering the boat back to shore.

For the next several weeks, Roy went aboard whaling steamers from the coast of Vancouver Island to as far north as Alaska taking photographs and recording as much information on whales as possible. He observed their swimming speeds, the amount of time they could spend underwater before coming to the surface, how many traveled together in a pod, and even witnessed their mating habits. When he was finished, he had amassed more first-hand scientific knowledge of whales

Men with beached whale, Amagansett, Long Island.

than had ever been collected before. He also purchased an entire whale skeleton and preserved dozens of vital organs for future study.

Roy returned to New York and found his superiors at the museum extremely pleased with the data he had gathered. Besides preparing the specimens and photographs for display, he also published several essays of his trip in newspapers and magazines, increasing public interest in whales and the museum. Roy soon became a recognized figure in the scientific community, and he even began giving lectures on his recent expedition to sold-out auditoriums and theaters.

Roy's work earned him a promotion, and several months later, the director called him into his office. When Roy entered, he sensed that something important was on Dr. Bumpus's mind. Roy took a seat in his usual chair and waited for his boss to begin speaking.

The director opened a manila folder, glanced at it, and slid it across his desk to Roy.

"I'll get right to the point, Andrews. The museum's board of trustees is quite satisfied with your recent excursion. They've therefore decided to extend our collections and displays of cetaceans and land mammals even further. Of particular importance to them is a part of the world that we have very little data on. So, I know it's short notice, but are you willing to take on another expedition?"

Roy could hardly believe his ears. Without another thought he replied promptly, "Yes, sir! I'm ready to go anywhere the museum would like to send me."

"That's what I thought, Andrews. That folder in front of you has all the information you need for arranging your transportation. And, start packing your bags. You leave next week. You're going to Asia this time—the Dutch East Indies. We want you to bring back as much data as possible, and you can send your specimens from any port in Asia directly to the museum by ocean liner."

Barely able to contain himself, Roy jumped to his feet and vigorously shook the director's hand. "Sir, I'll do my best. And, tell the board thank you for their vote of confidence."

Roy took the folder off the desk and strode out of the

office wearing a grin a mile wide. He ran all the way to his rented room uptown, packed his trunk, and called his parents. Only a few days later, he was on a train bound for Seattle and a ship waiting to carry him across the Pacific Ocean.

CHAPTER 7

MAROONED ON A TROPICAL ISLAND

ROY SAT AT HIS DESK IN HIS TINY CABIN hunched over a stack of books. He had been at sea for three days and was spending every available moment poring over descriptions of the flora and fauna of the Dutch East Indies. There were rare birds like the long-beaked hornbill that laid its eggs in the stumps of hollow trees, Sumatran tigers that stalked their prey through the dense jungles, and he even read several unconfirmed accounts of ferocious ten-foot long "dragon-lizards" that had attacked humans on the island of Komodo. Roy found little information on local cetaceans, however, and he hoped that his voyage would fill the gap in the scientific record on these important creatures.

In just a few days, Roy would complete his crossing of the ocean, and the ship would dock in Yokohama, Japan. He would join the *Albatross,* a vessel specially designed for scientific exploration, and sail southward to the East Indies. Roy knew he had no time to lose in researching his new destination and turned back to the books spread before him on the table.

He opened a history of the East Indies that he had grabbed from the museum library on the day he left New York. Roy was intrigued by this country composed of the largest chain of islands in the world stretching along the equator for almost 4,000 miles. He grew excited at the thought of visiting many of these faraway islands that had traded with Europe before America had even become a country.

Roy spent the rest of the crossing immersed in his books and touched land again in the Japanese port city of Yokohama. He transferred to another ship, sailed to the

Philippines, and arrived in the capital of Manila a couple of weeks later.

The first piece of news he received was that the ship that would take him through the Dutch East Indies was out of port. Roy decided that instead of lazing about the capital until the ship arrived the next week, he would travel to an island only a day's sail away and begin his scientific explorations early.

Roy hired two Filipino brothers, Heraldo and Mirando, to be his assistants. Early one morning, they caught a small boat to the island and after anchoring in the lagoon the three men waded through the surf with their gear. Dropping their equipment on the white sand under a stand of palm trees they waved good-bye to the captain. He would return in five days, and in the meantime, Roy and his men had a lot of work to do.

After making camp on the beach, Roy set about exploring the island. Most of it was covered in dense jungle interspersed with trickling streams and waterfalls. For hours, he crept through the brush, his khaki shirt and cargo pants becoming drenched with sweat.

Despite the tropical heat and the insects that buzzed around him, he walked as silently as possible. He didn't want to alarm the animals that he would come back to hunt the next day.

For the rest of the week, Roy walked over every inch of the island shooting and capturing dozens of rare birds, lizards, and rodents that would add to the museum's collection of Asian animals. At the end of every day of hunting, Roy would return to camp and work with his assistants long into the night preparing the specimens for the long sea journey back to the museum. On their fifth day on the island, they finished their work in the early afternoon and sat in the sand waiting for the ship to appear over the horizon. Roy lay on the beach drifting off to sleep, satisfied that his voyage had started out so well.

He was jolted from his brief nap by his assistant Heraldo. He looked up and saw that Heraldo was squatting next to him, gently shaking his arm. Roy rubbed his eyes and scanned the darkening sky.

"Sir," Heraldo whispered, "The ship not here. What to do?"

Roy raised himself to his feet. His two assistants looked worried, and he was slightly puzzled himself. He knew that he had to remain calm, though, or Heraldo and Mirando might panic. Surely this was only a short delay, he thought.

Roy thought for a minute and turned to his two assistants. "We better make a signal fire, just in case the ship's crew can't locate us in the dark. They're probably on their way right now, and we want to make sure they find us quickly."

The three men gathered dried coconuts and palm fronds and soon had an enormous fire blazing on the beach. They sat down near the roaring flames and contemplated their next move with an eye on the horizon. After waiting in silence for more than an hour, the two Filipino men began to grow anxious. Finally Mirando, Heraldo's younger brother, caught Roy's attention.

"What now, sir?" he nervously asked.

Roy eyed his two assistants through the dancing orange light of the fire. He saw the tension on both of their faces and knew he had to reassure them even though he had no idea when, or if, the ship would ever arrive.

"What now, Mirando? I'm sure they'll be getting to us shortly. It's got to be some minor mechanical problem or something. We'll be all right—we may just have to wait a bit."

And wait they did. The ship failed to show that night and the night after that. Roy's two assistants feared that the ship had capsized taking with it the only people who knew they were on the island. Roy remained calm, however, knowing that if this had happened, his contacts in Manila would eventually locate them. Besides, he now had a unique opportunity to live out a real-life version of his favorite boyhood story, *Robinson Crusoe*.

On the third day, when the ship had still not arrived, the three men decided to build a more permanent hut of palm wood and branches on the edge of the jungle. They transferred all of their equipment to their new shelter and took stock of their provisions. Despite careful rationing, they were down to their last few strips of dried meat and several handfuls of rice.

Roy reached for his gun and headed into the jungle in search of wild game. An hour later, Heraldo and Mirando heard shots from the other side of the island, and Roy shortly returned to camp with half a dozen pigeons slung over his shoulder. Heraldo roasted the birds over a bed of hot coals, and the men feasted into the night on the warm tender meat.

When Roy ran out of ammunition the next day, he showed his assistants how to make traps out of palm fronds and sticks and placed them throughout the jungle to catch small game. The men also speared crabs and fished in the lagoon using nets they had fashioned from thin jungle reeds. Mirando and Heraldo harvested salt by collecting seawater in a shallow pan and letting it evaporate in the sun.

With the abundance of food, the three men soon began to feel even more comfortable than they did on the ship. When the ship was still nowhere in sight they ceased worrying about being rescued and enjoyed relaxing on their tropical paradise. Finally after two weeks, they saw the boat appear over the horizon, and with some disappointment began packing their things for the trip back to civilization.

The boat drifted into the bay and anchored in the shallow water only a few hundred yards from their camp. The captain jumped into the lagoon, frantic that the delay had caused the men to starve to death on the island. He spotted them and raced across the beach, but when he arrived under the palm tree where they were sitting, he couldn't believe his eyes. Roy, Heraldo, and Mirando were lounging comfortably in the shade, polishing off coconut shell bowls brimming with fish and pigeon stew.

"Would you like to join us for a spot of lunch?" Roy asked, as if the men had casually bumped into each other at a restaurant in New York City.

"Thank God you're alive!" the captain said taking Roy's hand. "But, how on earth did you manage to survive? I'll bet you'll be glad to get back to Manila!"

"There's no hurry, captain. Have some lunch first. We'll have plenty of time to talk on the boat ride home."

The captain sat down and was offered a coconut shell

from Heraldo. He could clearly see that these castaways were in no hurry to leave paradise. He looked around the beach and saw the sturdy hut underneath the palm trees and the animal traps lying in the brush. He then peered back at the three relaxing contentedly in the sand beside the crystal clear water. It no longer seemed that the castaways were eager to return to the crowds and traffic of the capital.

TYPHOON

ROY ARRIVED BACK IN MANILA AND FOUND his ship in port waiting to begin the voyage to the Dutch East Indies. He spent a couple of busy days purchasing food and equipment and then set sail once again. For the next three months he explored countless secluded islands and visited the tranquil port cities of the Dutch empire.

Despite the months at sea, Roy couldn't fulfill his primary mission of documenting any new cetaceans, but he was able to catalog hundreds of mammals and fish and even discovered several new species of insects. As he neared the end of his trip Roy examined the crates of specimens that he had collected. He knew that his superiors at the museum, and especially its president, Henry Fairfield Osborn, whom he greatly admired, would be extremely pleased with his discoveries.

One of the last places Roy explored during his trip through the Dutch East Indies was the island of Borneo. When the ship docked to take on coal and supplies, Roy convinced the captain to stay in port for an extra week and he headed directly into the interior with Mirando.

After only a few hours in the jungle, Roy found that navigating through the thick vines and thorny brush was nearly impossible. He hacked at the dense foliage with his razor sharp machete but made little headway. He and Mirando were ready to quit when by chance they found a well-trodden game trail that led out of the brush.

Roy and Mirando continued along the trail and it soon expanded into a wide path surrounded by large banyan trees covered in long creeping lianas. The top branches of the trees created a dense canopy that nearly blotted out the rays of the afternoon sun. As they hiked along the cool jungle pathway, they were amazed to observe a wider variety of animals than they had seen in the rest of the islands. In just their first day, they observed orang-utans and macaques, several species of long-beaked hornbill birds, intricately-colored butterflies, and even the rare Sumatran rhinoceros and large-horned Sambar deer.

When evening approached, Roy began to consider where they would camp for the night. He was just about to stop to clear a space for their tent under a tall banyan tree when he was suddenly yanked back by his shirt collar and tumbled to the ground.

"What in God's name did you do that for?" Roy yelled, rubbing his shoulder where it had hit the ground.

Mirando didn't respond. He only put a finger to his lips and slowly pointed above their heads. Roy gazed up at a branch extending over the trail. He jumped to his feet when he saw an enormous brown python as thick as a man's leg slithering directly above the place where he had been setting up camp. The scales on its body gleamed in the late afternoon light and its forked tongue darted in and out menacingly as it sensed the air for prey. Roy was dumbfounded by the size of the snake. If Mirando hadn't noticed it and pulled him back an instant before, it would have surely dropped onto him, coiled its body around his torso, and constricted him to death.

"You shoot him . . . quick," were the only words Mirando could manage as he trembled in fright. The snake had already sensed their presence and was now dipping its head below the branch. Roy saw that its body was tensed and ready to fall on whatever was unlucky enough to pass beneath it.

Roy lifted his rifle and pulled the trigger. At the deafening sound of the gun, hundreds of jungle birds screeched in terror and took flight. The snake's head took a direct hit, and the enormous beast dropped to the jungle floor. It convulsed violently, tearing through the underbrush and whipping its powerful tail back and forth. Roy and Mirando jumped behind a tree stump and squatted there until the snake's death throes finally ended. When they were sure the snake was dead, they emerged and found it in the brush only a few feet from the trail. Its head had been ripped open by Roy's bullet, and it now lay flopped against its body, hanging by a thin strand of sinew.

Mirando calmly walked to the tail and stretched the snake until it was fully extended. Roy measured it and found that it was nearly ten feet long. The two men stood quietly in the brush in awe of the snake's massive size. Roy patted Mirando on the shoulder. He knew that if it hadn't been for his friend's sharp eyes, he would have been the one lying dead on the jungle floor.

The scientific research ship Alabatross.

Roy hiked through the jungle for another two days—wisely with Mirando leading the way. Then the two men headed back to the ship, so they could begin the return leg of the journey to Japan. After a brief stop in the Philippines to say good-bye to Heraldo and Mirando, Roy decided to stop at the island of Formosa, later known as Taiwan, before continuing on to Japan. Roy explored the island for a week, and although he was able to collect only a few specimens, he greatly enjoyed its tropical climate and peaceful villages.

On the day of his departure from Formosa, Roy secured his specimen crates in the ship's hold and walked up to the deck to bird-watch and read. After only a couple of hours, the sky turned dark, and it began to rain.

As Roy got up from his chair, a sharp gust of wind sent his hat flying over the railing. He hurried to get inside, and as he made for the door of his cabin, he spotted a large black rainsquall covering the horizon.

At that moment, a siren blared throughout the ship,

and the captain's voice reverberated over the loud-speaker.

"All hands to the bridge, all hands to the bridge. Typhoon ten miles off the port bow."

Roy ran to the front of the ship and into the control room. Fat droplets of rain were now thumping against the front windows as the sailors maneuvered the ship through the oncoming storm. Roy watched the captain lower his binoculars and focus on a large nautical map set against the bulkhead. He was so absorbed in dealing with the storm that he hadn't noticed Roy standing only a few feet behind him.

Roy cleared his throat to catch the captain's attention. "How serious is this going to be, captain?" he asked. "Do you think we need to head back to Formosa?"

The captain turned from the map. "Ah, Roy, I was just wondering about you. Join me. We've got quite a situation on our hands."

Over the last several months, Roy had come to deeply admire the captain. He was nearly seventy, but his boundless energy made him seem half his age. His steadfast courage had saved the ship, and Roy's life, more than a few times during the voyage. Roy stood next to him and listened as the captain traced his finger along the map.

"A few hours ago, we thought the typhoon would head north, but now it looks like it's going to blow right over us," the captain said, scratching his bristly white crew cut. "The winds will probably be at least ninety miles an hour. I just took a look at the map here, and I think it's best that we break for shore instead of trying to ride it out. If we're lucky, we'll make it to Keelung without much damage. You can stay and watch if you like, Roy, but I promise you, things are going to get bumpy."

As soon as the words left the captain's mouth, the ship plunged downward, almost knocking everyone on the bridge off their feet. Roy and the captain grabbed the wall railing, and a moment later the ship returned to an even keel. Jagged bolts of lightning were bursting from the clouds and striking the surface of the ocean. Water sprayed hundreds of feet into the air.

The captain turned back from the windows, and

though he tried to project a sense of calm throughout the bridge, Roy saw that his brow was furrowed with the gravity of the situation. He steadied himself and addressed the crew:

"Boys, we're going to get a direct hit from this storm on our way back to Formosa. I want all life jackets on from this moment forward. We're only about fifty miles from shore, but that doesn't mean we're going to get out of this unscathed. If God forbid we go down, I want you to know that it's been a pleasure serving with all of you."

The officers turned the ship about at the captain's order, and they began steaming back to the island. For the next hour, the ship sped through the choppy swells and rain. The approaching typhoon soon caught the vessel in its grip, however, and the drastically increasing wind rocked it back and forth.

Roy saw that the waves pounding against the boat were more than ten feet high. His knuckles turned white as great sheets of water blew up from the sea and drenched the deck below.

As the storm intensified, the bridge turned eerily calm as the men willed the ship ever closer to shore. Now that they were only twenty miles from land, Roy could see the square sails of Chinese fishing junks that had been caught out of port in the sudden storm. He watched as two of the boats not far away had their masts snapped like toothpicks by the howling gusts of wind. A massive wall of water whipped across the surface of the ocean and engulfed the fragile bobbing ships, sweeping the half dozen fishermen clinging to the decks into the violent foaming waves.

Even though they were right next to the boats, Roy and the crew were powerless to help the men. Their own ship was barely staying afloat, as every few minutes an enormous white-capped wave would slam into the bow and threaten to capsize the ship.

After fighting the typhoon for another six excruciating hours, they finally inched their way back to the port of Keelung in the middle of the night. The crew had to stay onboard as the typhoon continued to rage across the island. When the storm had finally passed out to sea, Roy and the captain emerged from the bridge. A quick tour of the ship showed them that they had been lucky to survive. It had sustained extreme hull damage and one of the engines had become clogged with seawater during the night. If they had stayed out even a few hours longer, the captain mentioned, they might have ended up at the bottom of the sea.

The men soon learned that dozens of boats had capsized when their wooden hulls could not withstand the fierce strength of the typhoon. Hundreds of people on the island had also died and entire villages had been obliterated by the high winds.

After a week of repairs, however, the ship was seaworthy again, and with weather conditions clear, Roy and the crew sailed to Japan. In just two days, they arrived in the bustling southern harbor town of Nagasaki.

As Roy excitedly walked ashore, he was captivated by the scene surrounding him. His voyage through the East Indies had been remarkable, but after only a few minutes, Roy sensed there was something unique about

Japan. He walked down the pier and paused on the boardwalk, breathing in the exotic scents of the street. The energy of the mass of people surrounding him filled the air like electricity, and he knew that it would be impossible to return to New York before he explored this fascinating country.

CHAPTER 9

SHARKS AT SEA

ROY JOURNEYED NORTH TO THE TOWN OF Aikawa on Sado Island, where there was a major whaling station. He knew the museum would allow him to stay in Japan if he continued his valuable research on cetaceans.

During his time in Aikawa, Roy made tremendous progress. He often spent sixteen-hour days cataloging and measuring various kinds of whales before they were stripped of their meat, baleen, and blubber for sale in the markets of Nagasaki and Tokyo.

At the end of work each day, he would stroll home through the town's back alleys and draw stares from the curious locals. Whenever Roy had time, he would call out to the villagers to join him for a quick chat; after hearing him speak Japanese, they would flock around him and follow him home, amazed that this tall *gaijin* (foreigner) could converse in their language.

During his stay in Aikawa, Roy also became friendly with a Norwegian captain and his crew. They had come to train several Japanese employees in harpooning and ship maintenance, but their job was nearly finished and they would soon return home to Europe.

A week before their departure, the captain invited Roy to go harpooning with them. Roy had been on the ship several times to observe whales just outside of the bay but this would be his first hunting expedition since he arrived in Japan. After breakfast, he walked down to the docks and jumped aboard the Norwegian whaling vessel. He greeted the captain and the other three whalers, and a few minutes later, the ship's ropes were loosened, and they set out to sea.

An hour later, the captain sighted a large humpback and began tracking it with his binoculars. Soon, it sprayed a funnel of water through its blowhole, and then dove into the ocean. The captain continued along the same bearing and the whale surfaced again five hundred yards directly in front of the boat. The captain pushed the throttle to full speed while one of the whalers stepped to the bow and attached a chain to the boat's harpoon gun. When they were only two hundred yards away, they saw the whale arch its massive fifty-foot long body and dip its head below the surface, poised to dive again.

"Fire away!" the captain roared from the bridge. "If we don't shoot now, we'll lose 'er!"

The whaler squeezed the trigger. Roy watched as the long spear sailed through the air, the thin metal chain trailing behind it. A second later, the harpoon curved downward and its tip splashed through the water before striking through the whale's back.

The harpoon penetrated almost a foot into the whale's body, but the beast barely shrugged. It resumed its dive and swam away from the ship tensing the chain attached to the harpoon. When the whale had towed out nearly a half-mile of chain, the captain ordered a full stop.

"Send out the rowboat," he ordered, shouting through

the window to his first mate at the bow. "We haven't got time to follow this thing all night. Let's get her ashore as fast as we can."

The first mate walked to the starboard gunwale and lowered the small wooden boat by hand crank into the water. He opened a long red box next to the crank and removed a second harpoon. Steadying the weapon in his right hand, he carefully began to climb down the rope ladder hanging from the side of the ship.

Roy watched from the bridge and knew that if he didn't follow him now, he might never get another chance to see a whale this close in the wild. He asked if he could join the other whaler in the rowboat.

"Permission granted," the captain answered. "If you do the rowing, that'll be a big help to Eriksen. Just make sure you don't stick around that whale too long when he finishes the job. I want you two back on the boat a.s.a.p."

"Aye, Captain," Roy smiled. He then darted out of the bridge and climbed down the ladder into the boat. Eriksen looked surprised, but then smiled at Roy while he steadied the heavy steel harpoon in his right hand.

"Just row up nice and steady," he began. "As soon as I throw the kill shot, you get us outta there instantly. If we linger a second too long, well, my ugly mug is the last one you'll ever see."

Despite Eriksen's attempt at humor, Roy could only bring himself to nod silently as he slowly backed away from the ship. He began rowing out to the whale in long strokes, dipping the oars soundlessly into the water.

A light wind helped carry the boat across the water, and Roy soon pulled up alongside the whale, the oars nearly brushing its side. The first harpoon was sticking out of the whale's back only a few feet away, and Roy could see the thick trail of blood dripping into the ocean. The whale was now lying still, exhausted from towing the ship's harpoon. Eriksen gestured for Roy to maneuver closer to the whale's body, and he rowed until the small boat bumped softly against the rubbery wet skin of its massive belly.

Roy rested the oars in the water and sat tensed as Eriksen slowly rose to a squatting position. He hefted the harpoon in his clenched fist, drew it back above his shoulder and, without a moment's hesitation, plunged it deep into the whale's stomach. The whale moaned with a dull roar that shook the boat, and its body began shuddering back and forth, churning the water around them into white foam. Roy attempted to escape from the gyrating beast but when he started to row away, the whale shook its body in the direction of the boat, snapping the right oar like a toothpick.

Now that it was impossible to flee, Eriksen and Roy gazed up at the whale, knowing that they were at its mercy. Eriksen gestured for them to dive into the water to try and swim back to the ship, but just as Eriksen leaned over the gunwale, Roy saw the whale heave its rotund body above the surface of the water. Its shadow covered the tiny rowboat, and the two men were frozen to their seats, too stunned to try and avoid their oncoming death. The whale crashed down into the sea, nearly drowning them in a massive wall of water.

The splash struck the men with such force that they were slapped against the bottom of the boat. Roy spat up seawater and wiped the salt from his eyes just in time to see the whale whip its ten-foot long tail skyward. It hovered above the boat for a second, and then the whale swiftly brought it down against the side of their boat, shattering it to pieces. The men plunged into the churning sea and Roy lunged for one of the boat's splintered planks before being sucked downward.

The piece of wood saved Roy's life as it helped him float upward after spending nearly a minute below the surface. While he clung to the plank, he vomited the seawater out of his lungs and began treading water. He then turned and saw the whale, its body coated in coagulated blood, slowly dive below the surface for what would likely be its last time.

After the whale had descended, Roy struggled to keep his head above the waves as he clutched the flimsy piece of wood. He heard a splash behind him, and saw Eriksen break the surface of the water. Thankful to see his shipmate alive, Roy swam toward him, but only a few seconds later, he spotted a pair of dark grey shapes sticking up from the waves. He stopped in mid-stroke, and when he saw what was heading toward them, he grabbed his wooden plank tightly to his chest and hung suspended in the water trying to keep as silent as possible.

"What is it?" Eriksen spluttered after spitting out a mouthful of seawater.

"Just turn around . . . slowly." Roy whispered. Eriksen's eyes nearly popped from his skull when he saw what was heading toward them. There were two ominous looking fins gliding through the water. The men could see that in less than a minute, the sharks would be upon them.

"Roy, there's three more coming up behind you!" Eriksen pointed across the water. Roy whipped his head around and saw that the three sharks had already begun circling less than twenty feet behind them. Roy turned back and saw that the first two sharks were now darting back and forth in the water, frenzied by the scent of the whale's blood. The two men looked at each other and knew that if they weren't rescued immediately, they would be eaten alive. They saw that the ship was now heading toward them, and the two men waved their arms hoping that the captain would arrive as quickly as possible.

A minute later, the boat pulled alongside Roy and Eriksen. The captain leaned his head over the gunwale and stared down at the two men struggling for their lives in the open sea.

"All right boys, keep your shirts on!" the captain began. "We're gonna tow the whale in, and then we'll be back to get you."

Roy turned to Eriksen in disbelief, and then shouted up to the captain.

"Are you crazy! We're going to be eaten alive here, and you're leaving us, so you can tow in a damn whale?"

"Just stay calm, and we'll be right back." The captain then signaled his navigator, and the ship drifted away from Roy and Eriksen. The two men then heard the low hum of the winch in the distance as the chain began pulling in the whale. In the meantime, they tried to avoid the sharks by remaining as still as possible in the water. At one point, Roy panicked when he felt the raspy, sandpaper skin of a shark brush across his leg as it swam past him. After what seemed like an eternity, the ship finally returned, and the captain lowered the ladder to the two desperate men. Roy and Eriksen pulled themselves up and collapsed on the deck exhausted, thankful that they had been lucky enough to stay alive.

The captain walked over to the two bedraggled men and eyed them through his wafting pipe smoke. "You see, I told you that you'd be all right. Back when I was a first mate, I was cast overboard myself and had to fend off the sharks for hours until the captain even realized I was gone! And, in all that time, I only got this little nip from the buggers." The captain then held out his left hand, showing Roy and Eriksen the stumps where his pinky and ring fingers had been bitten off.

He chuckled to himself and walked back to the bridge to steer the ship home. Still drenched, Roy and Eriksen headed below deck to dry off. They found an empty officer's cabin, and Eriksen made for the tiny bathroom while Roy stretched out on the bottom bunk. Eriksen toweled off and donned a neatly pressed officer's uniform that he found hanging on the bathroom door. When he emerged, he found Roy sound asleep on the bed, his clothes still dripping seawater onto the floor.

A few weeks later, Roy received a telegram from the museum requesting a progress report. Roy was tempted to write back saying that he would need another several months to complete his research, but as he had already examined every species of cetacean in Japan dozens of times and had enough of whale hunting for now, he had to admit that his mission was now accomplished.

CHAPTER 10

HIKING AND HUNTING
IN YUNNAN

WHEN ROY RETURNED TO NEW YORK CITY, HE discovered that his recent voyage had made him one of the most popular employees at the museum. Universities around the country also invited him to lecture on his expeditions, and he gave interviews to reporters wherever he traveled.

Roy grew accustomed to his recently earned fame and soon received a promotion as the assistant director of the museum's mammal collections. With his growing responsibilities, he found himself spending more time with the museum's president, Henry Fairfield Osborn. Both men had similar active, outgoing personalities and the two quickly became friends.

As the next couple of years passed by, though, Roy couldn't help thinking back to his past adventures. He was still not yet thirty, and he knew that his next big decision would shape his future career as an explorer.

While thinking of what new direction he might take, his life took a surprising turn. At one of the Manhattan parties he attended nearly every weekend, he met a young woman named Yvette who had just returned from studying in Europe. During their first conversation that evening, Roy learned that she was fluent in three languages and friends with several of the most illustrious royal families in France and Germany. They began courting and several months later were married.

Soon after their wedding, the idea that Roy had been looking for struck him like a bolt of lightning. He was in the Museum's auditorium, attending a lecture given by Osborn on the relatively new subject of evolution. This scientific theory, which had been first proposed by

Charles Darwin almost fifty years earlier, was still a revolutionary concept.

As Roy knew, the theory stated that all living things try to adapt to their environment as capably as possible. The animals that survive the best are the ones most likely to give birth and pass down their characteristics to the next generation. Over a long period of time, the species then gradually becomes better suited to its environment. For example, land animals might develop stronger legs for running, or keener eyesight for hunting prey. Certain fish would grow bigger fins for swimming or camouflage-like skin to disguise themselves from predators. In the case of humans, apes slowly evolved over thousands of years as they grew larger brains, shed their hair, and began to walk upright.

Although the theory made sense to most people, it remained controversial, as there was still a lack of scientific evidence to support Darwin's claims. Osborn was one of evolution's main proponents and he and Roy had had many discussions on the topic. In particular, Osborn often mentioned his own theory that mammalian life and humankind had originated on the plateaus of Central Asia. He offered the evidence that many species of mammals had emerged at the same time in both Europe and America. Therefore, they must have originated at a point in between, namely Central Asia. Osborn also theorized that early primates had migrated from this part of Asia to the rest of the globe and evolved into homo sapiens—better known as humans.

As soon as the lecture finished, Roy raced down to the podium and asked his friend to meet with him to discuss the exciting idea that had just popped into his head.

"What is it, Roy?" Osborn asked. By the look in his eyes, Osborn knew that his young colleague had stumbled onto something.

"Henry, this is going to be big—bigger than anything we've ever done. But, I can't explain here. I'll need to show you in my office. Are you free now?"

"After you," Osborn said as he packed up his briefcase and followed Roy out of the auditorium.

When they arrived at his office, Roy reached behind his filing cabinet and pulled out a long map rolled into a thick tube. He spread it out on his desk letting the corners drape over the sides. It was a map of Asia, and Roy stuck his finger at an unnamed point to the northwest of China.

"It just occurred to me, Henry. Why don't we actually launch an expedition to Central Asia to find evidence that supports your theory? You've been saying for years that the evidence is there just waiting to be discovered, but no one's dared make the effort. Just think of the publicity it would bring to the museum if we found the origins of ancient man and the earth's major land mammals. It would be unbelievable."

Osborn's eyes glowed. He knew it was the right time for an expedition of this magnitude. And, in his mind there was no better person to lead it. He made his decision then and there.

"We've just received some rather large donations to the museum. I can give you fifteen grand, and we'll fundraise the rest."

"Fantastic, Henry!" Roy reached out and vigorously shook Osborn's hand. "I think we can be ready in just a few months. I'll handle all the arrangements. Yvette will join me of course. She'll be in charge of photography."

"Excellent, Roy. I'll inform the board of directors tomorrow morning. But, there's just one detail I should mention. No one has yet successfully conducted an extensive scientific study in the heart of Central Asia and made any kind of headway. It's just too remote, and we don't quite know yet where we should even begin the hunt."

"So, what do you suggest, sir?" Roy asked, eyeing the map.

"Perhaps we could launch a series of expeditions. The first one might just be to scout the area and find out where to start. We might also want to collect some sample mammal specimens to see what the evolutionary record in Asia looks like.

"I think we should start on the Tibetan plateau, but in a more accessible area. Yunnan would be perfect."

Roy looked at the map and traced his index finger around the southwestern province in China. Osborn was right. It would be an excellent starting point and relatively easy to explore. Roy looked back at Osborn who was stroking his mustache and looking at the map.

"Sir, in six months, we'll be off to Yunnan."

"I know you will, Roy. The museum will be fully behind you. This expedition will make history."

On March 28, 1916, just a day less than six months later, Roy and Yvette set off aboard an ocean liner from San Francisco. After a long crossing of the Pacific, they landed at a port on the coast of China and drove into the capital of Beijing. As soon as their convertible entered the gates of the city, they were enveloped in swirling clouds of dust. With the persistence of their driver, they managed to locate their hotel, but could not leave the grounds for the rest of the day while the fine sand blew through the city. It was a storm, Roy thought, which symbolized the chaos currently engulfing the country.

Only five years earlier, the royal dynasty, which had controlled China for more than two centuries, finally collapsed from corruption and poor government. After the empire disintegrated, many Chinese hoped that the ensuing democratic revolution would stabilize the country. Rather than cooperating for the benefit of the nation, however, powerful men with private armies started battling for control and China descended into turmoil. When Roy arrived in Beijing, he wondered if the constant fighting between these warlords would make it too dangerous to continue.

Roy ultimately decided that he had invested too much effort to abandon the expedition and decided to press on. He figured that things would proceed safely once they arrived in South China.

Roy and Yvette sailed for Hong Kong and met their old hunting companion and friend, Edmund Heller. The three then hired an interpreter named Wu Hung Dao who quickly proved that he not only spoke excellent English, but also was remarkably resourceful. He took them outside of the city and helped them purchase two dozen horses to carry the enormous amount of cargo that they would transport over the Yunnan Mountains. They hired porters, a cook, and several ex-soldiers who would serve as guards in bandit-infested territory. Wu negotiated the prices very carefully. In China, there was no set price for anything, and if someone wanted a good deal, he had to be a shrewd bargainer.

After leaving Hong Kong, they journeyed overland and sailed by flat-bottomed sampans down a series of rivers until they arrived in Yunnan, meaning "south of the clouds" in Chinese. As they traveled through the first few miles of the province, they saw how the name had originated. The rivers were surrounded by tall craggy mountains that were covered in thick puffy clouds. There were mud brick houses clinging to the sides of the steep gorges, but they only appeared in the heat of the day after the morning fog had lifted.

Once they began exploring Yunnan, Roy felt that he had entered a different country. The province contained more than two dozen ethnic groups, and the people spoke languages that were much different from Chinese. They were dressed in brightly colored robes and jackets and some of the women wore elaborately styled head-dresses decorated with jewelry and braided cloth.

Roy's horse caravan traveled along decrepit and slippery stone roads for another week until they gratefully arrived in the town of Dali where they were finally able to rest. They camped at the side of a lake, and as night began to fall, they noticed an unusual spectacle. The surface of the water had become illuminated with lights. Roy strolled to the edge of the lake and saw that there were dozens of thin reed boats each with a flaming torch tied upright to the bow. In the middle of each boat stood a man propelling himself across the lake with a long bamboo pole. Roy then noticed something rather strange. On the edge of each boat were two large beaked cormorants that flapped their wings up and down but seemed in no hurry to take flight.

Roy peered through his binoculars and though it was almost dark, he saw that the necks of the birds were tied to the side of the boat with long thin ropes. He watched as the birds dove headfirst down into the water, and a minute later broke the surface to fly back to the boat. Roy was amazed to see that in each of their beaks was a large twitching whitefish! He had heard that cormorants were excellent fishers, and he now understood that the ropes around their necks had prevented them from swallowing their catch. It was without a doubt the most interesting method of fishing he had ever seen.

The party spent the next several days resting in Dali, and then set out into the forests of Yunnan to hunt and trap. For two months, Roy, Yvette, and Edmund captured all kinds of animals and even trapped dozens of rodents to help study how the mammals of Asia had evolved. Each night, they camped in a different place and enjoyed their meals with the fine wine they had packed from Hong Kong. The three passed the evenings playing cards, taking photographs, or recording the day's adventures in their journals.

They eventually made their way north and soon found themselves ascending the high plateaus that led into Tibet. As their long caravan wound its way up and down the steep slopes, they began seeing Tibetan nomads clad in thick sheepskin robes on horseback. These men were headed for the small bustling market towns in the valley below. There they would barter large sacks of salt that they had collected from vast dried-out lake beds for barley, the daily Tibetan staple, and other necessities needed to live in their high altitude camps. As Roy and the others passed them on the trail, the Tibetan horsemen stuck their tongues out and playfully smiled.

"Why on earth are they doing that?" Roy asked Wu. "Don't they like us or something?"

"Oh, sir, this is just their way of greeting you. They're being polite!"

Roy shook his head in laughter. Wherever he traveled

Yvette Andrews feeding a baby bear.

in the world, he was always amazed seeing the practices of other cultures so different from his own.

The next week, Roy, Yvette, and Edmund were relaxing in the dining tent after a long day's ride when they heard Wu scamper up and stick his head through the flap.

"Mr. Andrews, we've got a problem! The local warlord sent some of his soldiers to collect his tax. They said we won't be able to pass unless we give them six of our horses! Our men are angry, sir. They kindly ask that you give them permission to . . . how do you say? They desire to . . . break their heads."

"Break their heads?" Roy asked surprised.

"Yes, sir. If they don't, the warlord and his soldiers will follow us until we're back in Dali and then rob us blind. Besides, sir, our men are strong and ready for a fight."

Roy reached for his gun. "Should I . . ."

"That won't be necessary, sir. We'll handle it." Wu then strode away and began shouting commands in Chinese.

As Roy closed the tent flap, he heard the first blows of

the fight with the warlord's soldiers. For the next ten minutes the three sat in the tent as the soldiers yelped and begged for mercy at the hands of Roy's men. When the noise of the brawl finally died down, Roy emerged and found the soldiers kneeling on the ground. He promptly ordered them back to town, and they slowly rose to their feet with their arms in the air. With his rifle at his side, Roy watched as they staggered back down the trail rubbing the growing lumps on their heads and backsides.

The rest of the journey proceeded uneventfully, and they arrived back in Dali two weeks later. Roy, Yvette, and Edmund had managed to collect hundreds of specimens and surveyed huge portions of the countryside. But, the most important outcome of the trip was that Roy could now see how a major scientific expedition to Central Asia would be possible. As he sailed home to America, he began making preparations for his next journey. He was unaware at the time that his plans would drastically change, and world events would compel him to return to Asia much sooner than he anticipated.

CHAPTER 11

CODE NAME REYNOLDS

WHEN ROY'S SHIP DOCKED IN SAN FRANCISCO, he discovered that in his year-long absence, America had been transformed. The war in Europe, which had begun before he left, was the subject on everyone's lips. It would later be known as World War I and as Roy set foot on U.S. soil, thousands of American lives were being lost in the trenches of France every month. While he had been in Yunnan, Roy was able to follow the conflict through scattered news reports, but it was only now that he realized how widespread and disastrous the war was.

When he learned the extent of America's involvement in the war, Roy felt it was his patriotic duty to lend his services to his country. He informed Osborn at the museum of his desire to join the fight and then headed to Washington, D.C. to enlist in the armed forces. On his first day in the city, he stopped for lunch at one of the capital's exclusive social clubs. As he was dining alone, a man passed by his table and stopped dead in his tracks.

"Roy, is that you?"

Roy looked up from his food and saw that it was his old hunting companion, Charles Sheldon.

"Charlie, how are you! It's been ages, hasn't it? What are you doing in D.C.?"

"I might ask you the same question, old friend. Your recent expedition has been all over the papers. I'd think you'd be touring the country basking in your fame by now!"

"I'm afraid not, Charlie. If you can believe it, I've actually come down here to join the war effort."

Charles' eyes widened briefly before he pulled out a chair and sat across from his friend.

"You know, Roy, I've actually gotten involved myself. I'm doing some sensitive work for the government."

He then looked around the room and leaned over the table. "Intelligence work, Roy. And, it's a fantastic coincidence that I bumped into you. We've actually been desperate for an agent to monitor the political situation in the Far East. There are few men we can trust that have your experience, Roy. What do you say? You'd be doing your country a tremendous service."

Roy set down his napkin and waved for the check. "I've got only one question, Charlie. When do I leave?"

Less than a month later, Roy and Yvette were back in China, this time living in the capital, Beijing. They loved every minute in the thriving metropolis of people from all over China and around the world. Fancy restaurants and nightclubs were crowded with foreigners and wealthy Chinese every night of the week. Set amidst the modern sections of town were traditional neighborhoods of courtyard houses and twisting back alleys that had changed little in the past two centuries. But, with the conflict still raging in Europe and warlords fighting for control of the government, the once tranquil capital had become a freewheeling haven where refugees, secret agents, revolutionaries, and soldiers of fortune made their home.

Roy began his mission of monitoring foreign diplomats and spies while working under the cover of planning another expedition for the museum. Every few weeks, a letter with instructions from Washington would be secretly delivered to his home. Scrawled in the left corner of the envelope would be Roy's code name—Reynolds. The messages were written in invisible ink between the lines of ordinary letters from Charlie. To make the ink appear, Roy would heat the letter by slowly rubbing the paper over a light bulb. He would then decipher it using a code that he had memorized before leaving America.

In late 1918, just as the war in Europe began winding down, Roy received his most important letter yet. He was instructed to travel to Mongolia to investigate Russian influence in the capital city of Urga. Only a year earlier, Russia had undergone a Communist revolution and many in the U.S government worried that it would attempt to control other countries along its border.

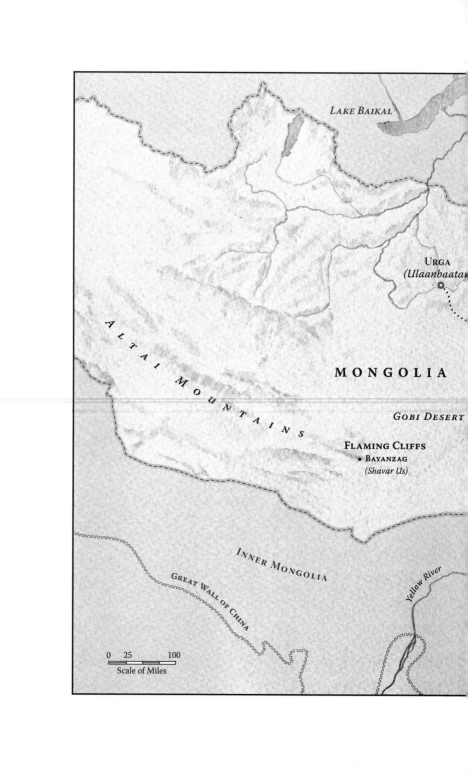

LAKE BAIKAL

URGA
(Ulaanbaatar)

MONGOLIA

GOBI DESERT

FLAMING CLIFFS
• BAYANZAG
(Shavar Us)

ALTAI MOUNTAINS

INNER MONGOLIA

GREAT WALL OF CHINA

Yellow River

0   25   100
Scale of Miles

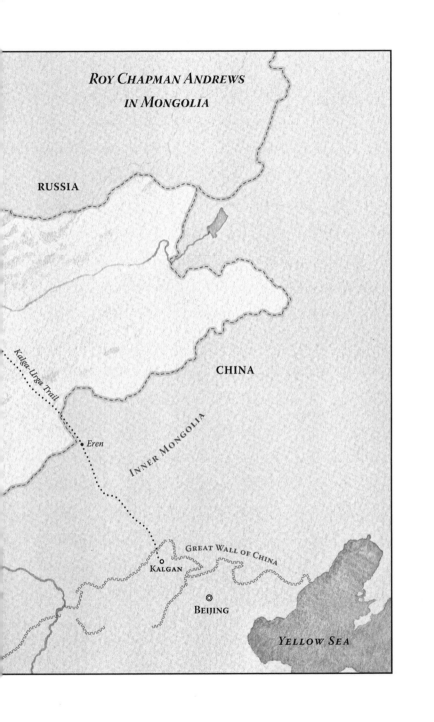

ROY CHAPMAN ANDREWS
IN MONGOLIA

RUSSIA

Kalga-Urga Trail

CHINA

INNER MONGOLIA

Eren

GREAT WALL OF CHINA

KALGAN

BEIJING

YELLOW SEA

Roy purchased a convertible motorcar and drove out of the city with his friend and longtime Beijing resident, Charlie Coltman. They spent their first day driving through Northern China and were soon traveling along a hardscrabble dirt road through the Gobi desert. In the late afternoon as they neared Mongolian territory, they approached a steep rocky hill on their right. Just as their car began to pass under its shadow, five men appeared on horseback at the top of the hill, leveled their guns and opened fire. Three shots landed in the sand in front of the car, but the other two hit the mark and struck their right rear door with a loud pop.

Completely taken by surprise, Roy yanked the wheel hard to the left and bounced off the road in a cloud of dust. As Roy tried to steady the wheel and steer over the rocky terrain, Charlie looked back to the top of the hill. Perched on their horses just below the fiery orange setting sun, the five bandits were cocking their rifles for another shot.

"Floor it, Roy! They're gonna shoot any second!" Charlie screamed over the sound of the roaring engine and wind. An instant later, Roy pulled the car back onto the main road, and they careened past the hillside. Roy reached into the backseat to grab his rifle for a quick shot at the bandits. At that moment, the second volley of shots rang out and one of the bullets shattered the lower half of the steering wheel where Roy's hands had been only a split second earlier. The car nearly spun out of control, and Roy grabbed the remaining part of the wheel and raced around a bluff on the left side of the road.

As Roy pulled out of sight of the bandits, the car suddenly slowed down and jolted to a stop. Roy looked over the hood and saw that the front tires had become mired in loose sand. Both men got out of the car and took a closer look.

"It's a trap, Charlie. I'll bet those first shots were just to scare us into hiding behind this bluff. Those bandits must have been there all day, just waiting for a car to pass. I'll bet they're taking their time now, Charlie. They must think they've caught a couple of flies in their spider web. But, we've still got a bit of luck on our side."

Charlie stared back at his friend. "Luck? We've got five

bandits bearing down on us in the middle of nowhere, and our car's stuck in a pile of sand. Pardon me, Roy, but I have a hard time seeing how that adds up to luck!"

"My friend, you're forgetting that we didn't have time to get a single shot off! They must think we're unarmed! They're probably taking their time right now coming over here thinking they can fleece us for everything we've got. They've got no idea what's in store for them."

"Good thinking, Roy. Now, I'm sure you know what we do next."

Charlie grabbed both rifles out of the back seat and tossed one to Roy. The men raced up the side of the bluff. When they reached the top a minute later, they ducked down next to a boulder for cover and looked over the sights of their guns. Charlie saw that Roy had been absolutely right. The five horsemen were casually trotting across the plain and talking to each other as if the two foreigners in the car were helplessly stuck in the sand, just waiting to be robbed.

Charlie whispered to Roy that he was ready to fire. They both took aim and pulled the trigger at the same time. Two bandits immediately dropped to the desert floor. The other three froze in shock. When they looked up and saw that their former victims now held the high ground, they didn't waste another second. They whipped their horses and took off across the desert in the other direction.

When the bandits disappeared over the horizon, Roy and Charlie walked back down the hill. They struggled to pull the car out of the sand, and after an hour of rocking it back and forth, they finally managed to wrench the car free. Roy took the wheel again, and they pressed on across the desert until nightfall. The two tired friends arrived at a Buddhist temple outside a small village and decided to stay the night. Before they went to bed, they had the head lama chant a special prayer to ensure they had similar luck for the rest of their journey.

Three days of hard driving later, Roy and Charlie arrived in the Mongolian capital. Urga was located in a lush green valley beside a forested mountain. They entered the city by driving across a wooden bridge over a wide flowing river, and when they reached Urga's main street, they marveled at the sites around them. Urga was the only city in the country and was quite small, but it contained a fascinating mixture of architecture and people. There were large neighborhoods of round white *ger* tents covering the valley and hills. Near the city center, there were rows of Chinese shops tightly crammed next to each other and small wooden houses surrounded by high picket fences. Next to the small town square, there were several two-story log cabins, which appeared to be government offices.

Roy and Charlie stopped the car outside Urga's largest structure—Gandan Buddhist monastery. They stood in front of the gate and viewed their first taste of daily life in the capital. Men wearing long *dell* robes rode stocky, large-headed horses down the street, stopping only to gaze at the unusual sight of a passing motorcar. Street hawkers squatted on their haunches in front of small cracked tables of tobacco and hard candies while their children played bone marbles next to them in the dirt. Mongolian women with hair pressed into wide bejeweled headdresses casually chatted in pairs, cracking pine nuts between their teeth.

As Roy and Charlie went to meet their contact in a compound next to the monastery, they saw half a dozen shaven headed, yellow robed lamas cross the street and enter the temple grounds. The lamas held their heads down in deep meditation and chanted in unison paying scant attention to the two white men waiting outside the front gate.

Roy spent the next two weeks assessing the political situation of the country and writing a report to send back to headquarters in Washington. He then left Urga, and spent an entire month traveling through the countryside. There he noticed that the open plains teemed with dozens of species of wild game. He drove along the outer edges of the Gobi desert and saw that it was filled with sedimentary rock formations and dried out riverbeds—perfect locations to dig for fossils and search for evolutionary clues of ancient mammals.

When Roy returned to Beijing, the war was drawing to

a close. By now he had fewer duties as Agent Reynolds, so he decided to cable Osborn and ask if the museum could fund an initial exploration trip to Mongolia. Roy still had plans for the major expedition that he had previously discussed with his mentor, but he wanted to be sure that Mongolia was the right country in which to make such a large investment of time and money. Osborn readily agreed with Roy's idea and wired him several thousand dollars. Roy wasted no time and a few weeks later, he, Yvette, Charlie, and several Chinese assistants departed Beijing in new motorcars bound for the open steppe of Mongolia.

The group spent the entire summer traveling through the Mongolian countryside by vehicle, horse, and camel. They journeyed east to film the herds of thousands of antelope galloping across the steppe. In the southwest, Roy and Charlie hiked through the Gobi-Altai mountain range hunting the big-horned Argali sheep. Yvette photographed dozens of herding families and filmed various cultural festivals. They also spent weeks camping in the desert, surveying the land and discussing with the locals the best points for future travel and exploration.

As they had done in Yunnan, Roy and Yvette collected hundreds of specimens and photographs. This time, however, Roy knew that the search for the location to prove Osborn's theory about evolution was over. Mongolia was the ideal choice for a major expedition. For everything to succeed, however, he'd need more than detailed planning and hard work. To get through the difficult experiences that surely lay ahead, Roy would have to rely on the lucky star that had shone down on him ever since he was a boy.

CHAPTER 12

CAMELS AND CARS CROSS THE DESERT

AS SOON AS HE WAS BACK IN NEW YORK, Roy headed to the museum to meet with Osborn. They celebrated his return over brandy and cigars, as Roy told stories of his journey to Mongolia. He excitedly spread a large map of Asia over Osborn's desk and began outlining his proposal of returning to Mongolia. He would call it the Central Asian Expeditions.

"You see, Henry," Roy said as he traced his finger across southern Mongolia. "As I mentioned before, the Gobi has an ideal environment for any paleontologist. Now some think that digging out there is hopeless because no one's found much so far. But, we've got an advantage. We can be the first to use motorcars to cross the desert. We'll cover ten times the amount of distance that any other explorer ever has on saddle alone."

"And supplies?" Osborn asked raising an eyebrow.

"Well, Henry, we're going to do it the Mongolian way. We'll hire a camel caravan to carry fuel for the cars and other supplies. The caravan will meet us at certain points along the route. We'll be able to stay mobile and explore a huge amount of territory."

Osborn looked up from the map and scratched his bushy mustache. He had been waiting for this type of daring expedition since he took the helm at the museum. It had long been his goal to enter the history books with an original scientific discovery. He realized, however, that many of his colleagues would surely criticize him for what they thought was a foolhardy undertaking. After all, little evidence of ancient life had ever been found in the Gobi. But he knew that if anyone had the audacity to pull off such a risky operation, it was the man standing right beside him.

"Roy, I've always put my faith in you. You know that. That's why we're going to do this expedition."

"Fantastic!" Roy said, shaking Osborn's hand. "I won't let you down."

"I know you won't, Roy." Osborn then paused and put a hand on his friend's shoulder. "But, if this is ever going to get off the ground, we're going to need an enormous amount of financing."

"I've thought of that too, Henry. I'm going to ask some of the museum's famous benefactors for funds. Once people see that America's most powerful men are donating, our expedition will become the cause of the season. The rest of the money should then roll in."

Roy spent the next several weeks visiting corporate offices and dining in the luxury apartments of Manhattan's elite. He soon obtained donations from such famous businessmen as J. P. Morgan Jr., the son of America's most influential banker, and John D. Rockefeller, one of the richest men in America and founder of the Standard Oil Company. Once the newspapers ran stories of the expedition and the influential men who had contributed, many of New York's upper class hastened to write checks to the museum, eager not to be left out of the most exciting event of the year.

Once Roy had reached his financial goals, he spent several months making preparations and assembling the team that would journey from Beijing to the Gobi desert. As the Central Asian Expeditions had become the most anticipated scientific voyage in decades, Roy was able to recruit some of the country's top scientists and field men to join him.

The chief scientist of the expedition worked just down the hall from Roy at the museum. Walter Granger was one of the world's leading authorities on prehistoric mammals, fossil collection, and preservation. Many at the museum thought that he was the perfect choice to serve as the expedition's deputy. He would balance Roy's devil-may-care attitude and constant need for activity with his calm personality and meticulous approach to fieldwork.

The expedition also included famous geologists and paleontologists such as Charles Berkey and Frederick

Morris. To record the events of their journey, Roy also hired the photographer J. B. Shackelford. As the expedition would rely on motor transport, he took on the young Bayard Colgate, heir to the Colgate-Palmolive fortune, who was an expert in vehicle maintenance. Other support staff such as cooks, porters and, most importantly, a reliable camel master, would be hired in China.

Roy was finally ready to leave in the spring of 1921. He would be traveling to Beijing with Yvette and once he

Stopping by a Chinese walled city to cool the motors.

established a headquarters for the expedition, the rest of the team would join them. In honor of his departure, Osborn held a good-bye party in the museum's conference room. After Osborn gave a toast, Roy was swarmed by journalists requesting interviews.

"Gentlemen, please!" Osborn said, thrusting his arms into the crowd. "You'll have plenty of time to talk to our boy before he leaves. But as his boss, I get the first word!" Osborn then playfully grabbed Roy's arm and led him out to the hallway.

When they were alone, Osborn looked Roy squarely in the eye.

"Let's put aside all that baloney that's going on in there for just a second. You must be nervous as hell."

Roy inhaled a deep breath. "I am, Henry. This is a mighty big gamble we're taking. If this fails, you'll lose your reputation, and I'll become a laughingstock."

"Roy, do you remember when you first started working here? You were mopping the floors, right?"

"Of course, Henry. How could I forget?"

"Well, even back then, Roy, you were an optimist.

Whenever we've talked, even back then, you've always told me you could do things that others said could never be done. The fossils are out there, Roy. Now, it's time for you to go and find them."

As soon as his car passed through the wall surrounding Beijing, Roy waved his hat jubilantly into the air. Every time he returned to the city, he felt its vibrant energy pulsing through his veins, and as he drove down Beijing's main street, the ancient sloping roofs of the capital seemed to reach out and welcome him. Roy realized there were grueling months of preparations ahead, but for now, he exulted in winding his way through the crowded streets of the old city. This dusty pulsating metropolis was his second home, and he knew that once the expeditions began, he would be returning here for many more years to come.

Once Roy settled into life in Beijing, his first order of business was finding a house to use as headquarters. He purchased a sprawling mansion in the center of town that had been previously owned by a prince. It contained dozens of rooms and was arranged in several compounds, each surrounding a large courtyard. There were also several garages, a horse stable, and quarters for the housekeepers and cooks.

When the house was ready, Roy began preparing for the expedition. Throughout the muggy Beijing heat of summer and fall, he spent much of his time indoors: planning logistics, studying Chinese, or obtaining necessary provisions and equipment. By the time winter came and the other members of the expedition began arriving in Beijing, the entire compound was stacked with hundreds of crates of canned and dried food, camping gear, and scientific paraphernalia.

In mid-March, just before they were ready to depart, Roy transported the gear to the small town of Kalgan north of Beijing. There he bought several dozen two-humped Bactrian camels and, with the help of his recently hired Mongolian camel master, Merin, and a small group of Chinese porters, the men strapped the hundred pound boxes to the camels' sides. When the camels were ready, Merin led them down the road and out through the towering gate of the Great Wall of China. A month later, if all went well, he would rendezvous with the expedition in the Gobi desert.

Roy had also purchased several cars in Kalgan and after all the members of the expedition arrived on the train from Beijing, they loaded their gear and were finally ready to set out. On the day they left, nearly the entire town turned out to watch as the vehicles sped off across the open plain.

CHAPTER 13

SANDSTORM

DESPITE ROY'S INITIAL FEAR THAT THE expedition would fail, it took less than a week to make their first discovery. On a hot, dusty day just outside of the border town of Eren, Roy decided to make camp early and cross into Mongolia the next day. Granger, Berkey, and Morris took a walk in the hills and didn't return until sunset. When they walked back into camp, the three scientists were grinning from ear to ear.

"What is it?" asked Roy. "You've found something, haven't you?"

Walter approached Roy and clutched his shoulders. "It's all here! "It's here, Roy! It's all here! This is just a sample." Granger then reached into his shirt pocket and held a closed fist out to Roy. He then slowly opened his palm to reveal several prehistoric mammal teeth and the chipped fragments of dinosaur bones.

"We've also discovered a rather large fossil. It's going to take some time to dig it up. We'll give that first priority tomorrow."

The men celebrated that night by roasting pheasants over an open fire and drinking a bottle of champagne. The next morning, Granger and Berkey rose early. When Roy arrived at the hillside where the two scientists were patiently working, he stopped dead in his tracks. He watched as Granger and Berkey carefully whittled away encrusted dirt from a beautifully preserved four-foot long dinosaur leg bone.

The men heard Roy approach, and Berkey gestured for him to crouch beside the bone in the sand.

"The bone here, Roy, is certainly from the Cretaceous," Berkey began. "We checked out the rocks on the other side, where we found those mammal teeth, and we've determined that those are from the Cenozoic. These finds are spectacular, but more important, they're the first fossils of these periods ever discovered in Asia. I never thought I'd live to see the real evidence, but good old Osborn and his theory that Asia is the mother of all life may be right after all."

Even though the fossils were millions of years old, Roy was certain that Granger and Berkey had accurately dated each specimen. The men had used the simple yet effective technique of determining the age of the dinosaur bones by analyzing the rock that surrounded them.

Most fossils around the world are found in sedimentary rock. Over long periods of time, dirt and minerals collecting on the ground form into sediment, eventually hardening into special layers of rock called strata. The strata then build horizontally giving the rock a lined appearance.

Once a fossil is discovered, the paleontologist inspects the strata by determining how far down in the rock the fossil was located—the lower in the rock, the older the fossil. By then measuring the length of time it takes for one layer of rock to form, the fossil can then be dated. The fossil may also be compared to identical specimens found in other places to determine if the date is accurate. When the Central Asian Expeditions began, more modern chemical dating methods were being developed, but the scientists in the Gobi still relied on this dependable technique.

Roy and his team spent the next few days at their camp in Eren, packing the fossils in fine paper and then encasing them in hard plaster casts for shipment back to

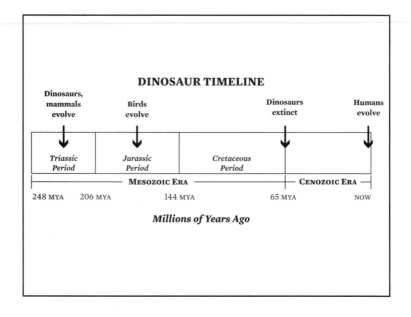

DINOSAUR TIMELINE

Dinosaurs, mammals evolve — Birds evolve — Dinosaurs extinct — Humans evolve

Triassic Period — Jurassic Period — Cretaceous Period

MESOZOIC ERA — CENOZOIC ERA

248 MYA — 206 MYA — 144 MYA — 65 MYA — NOW

Millions of Years Ago

New York. Then the men loaded their supplies back into the cars and crossed the border into Mongolia, driving along the edge of the Gobi desert.

They rode until they reached the sacred mountain of Tuerin just a couple hundred miles from Urga. It was here that Roy had instructed Merin to meet them with the camels. Once the men had arrived, they set up camp and began servicing the vehicles for the drive to the capital.

The next morning, just as Roy had started helping Colgate clean one of the car engines, he saw something appear in the distance. He squinted into the sunlight and saw the long unmistakable two-humped shadows cast across the sand. The camel caravan snaked its way over the dunes, and Roy and the others watched in amazement as Merin steered the long-necked beasts toward the mountain in a single file. Incredibly, Merin had driven the camels through hundreds of miles of forbidding desert, extreme heat, and marauding bandits and made it to the rendezvous only a day behind schedule.

After the team took on supplies from the camels, they drove off to Urga, agreeing to meet Merin and the caravan in the Gobi desert later in the expedition. Once they arrived in Urga, they spent an agonizing month waiting for permission from the authorities to explore the country. When their documents were ready, they headed directly to the Gobi.

For a week the men drove through the pebbly terrain and isolated shrubs of the desert. One day, they arrived at a well, which was surrounded by high, boulder-covered hills, and deep, dried-out riverbeds.

Several years earlier, when Roy was visiting Urga, a European scientist had mentioned to him that Mongolian nomads collected small dinosaur bones from the area and made a living selling them to Chinese dealers in the city. The Chinese had an enormous appetite for the fossils, as they believed the "dragon bones" had special healing properties if they were ground into powder and dissolved in hot water to be drunk as a tea.

The scientists began excavating for fossils and quickly discovered that the area was everything they had dreamed of. They found complete fossils of fish, insects, and small mammals that were tens of millions of years old. Roy also observed that the desert around them received enough rainfall to sustain a substantial amount of life. He documented small herds of gazelles, mountain goats, and wild camels and sighted dozens of great-winged vultures drifting through the air in long figure eights, scanning the ground for prey.

Roy even discovered a small, bizarre-looking rodent with long pointed ears and hind legs twice as long as its body. When the other members of the expedition examined it, they realized that it had never before been cataloged. In honor of Roy, they gave the animal the scientific name, *Stylodipus andrewsi*.

On their second day in camp, as the sun began its long slow descent into the horizon, the men gathered around a fire taking inventory of everything they had found so far. Just as Roy was finishing the task of jotting down each specimen that his team had found that day, he looked up from his journal. He noticed an empty chair next to the campfire. The smell of cherry pipe tobacco that usually wafted through the camp during the evenings was also missing.

"Has anyone seen Walter?" Roy asked.

"He was out digging with Shackelford, I think." Berkey replied. "He's not back yet? He's been out in that riverbed all day."

"All right, I'll drive out and . . . wait, that must be him coming over the ridge now."

A minute later, the car pulled up in front of the tents and Granger got out while Shackelford remained behind the wheel. Granger strode up to his colleagues sitting around the fire, and Roy noticed a broad smile curl under the fringes of his friend's mustache. He knew that Walter had made another discovery.

"We've got something, gentlemen," Walter announced. "Now if I can steal you away from your comfy chairs for just a few minutes, you might find this interesting."

The men piled into two cars and followed Shackelford and Granger until they neared a group of bare rocky hills several miles outside of camp. As the cars pulled up beside a pale jaggedly lined hillside, Roy could see a large bone peeking out of the dirt. He flung open the door and jogged to the base of the hill. As soon as he approached the bone, he saw that only a few feet away a long exposed vertebrae and the rounded dome of a skull were also in the initial stages of excavation.

"It's a *Baluchitherium*," Walter said when he caught up with Roy.

"Only a few others have ever been discovered. It's the largest land mammal in history. Just by looking at the bones here, you can see that it was over twenty feet tall and twenty-five feet long.

"I'd also be willing to bet that we'll find more fossils in the area if we just poke around. We've got some shards of unknown mammals next to the bones right here."

"Then what are we waiting for?" Roy said, scanning the base of the hillside. "Let's start digging."

"Hold on a minute there, Roy." Granger said. "What do you mean 'we'?"

Granger and the rest of the men had been wary of Roy's field technique ever since the expedition began. It was clear that he was a master of organization and a courageous leader, but his restless personality made him too impatient for the meticulous and time-consuming task of dinosaur bone collection. On one occasion, Granger had even seen him wrenching a delicate bone out of the ground with his bare hands, nearly splintering it in the process.

Roy chuckled back at Granger, knowing that his old friend was right.

"Fine. While you're clawing through the sand, I'll be out hunting for dinner. I wouldn't want to get in the way of your delicate work."

The team spent the next week painstakingly unearthing each section of the *Baluchitherium* while finding dozens of other fossils and dinosaur bones that lay just beneath the surface. On their last day at the site, while prospecting alone on the other side of the hill, Roy noticed a slight wind picking up and a dark cloud appear on the horizon. He grabbed his binoculars from his backpack and, after focusing the lenses, stared ahead in numb horror. The biggest sandstorm he had ever seen was heading directly toward him.

Roy watched the wall of sand churn across the desert floor, hoping that it might subside before it reached the hills where he was standing. Before he left Kalgan, Merin had told him about the fierce Gobi sandstorms. They could be fatal and, on occasion, they had wiped out nomadic families and their herds of animals.

Roy felt the wind whip at the collar of his shirt and realized the sandstorm was gaining strength. The men on the other side of the hill still hadn't seen the storm approaching, and if he didn't alert them immediately, it might be too late.

Roy circled the hill, pinching the brim of his hat tightly around his head to keep it from flying away in the strengthening wind. As soon as he saw the men, he began yelling and waving his arms.

"Sandstorm! Take cover, take cover!"

The men stood in shock, thinking that the wind they had felt was nothing more than a strong afternoon breeze. When they saw the look on Roy's face, though, they dropped their tools and ducked under a group of boulders at the bottom of the hill.

The storm was now getting closer, and the wind started howling as Roy raced to join the others. When he made it to the rocks, he squatted next to Walter, thankful he'd taken cover just as the sand began to beat down on them. Walter grabbed him by the arm and shouted into his ear over the sound of the wind.

"We've got to cover those dinosaur teeth we found out in the valley! The sand's going to tear them to shreds!"

"Forget it, Walter! If you go out into that sand, you'll be buried alive. We need you around to dig for fossils, not become one of them!"

"Sorry, Roy, but I've got no choice!"

Walter leapt to his feet and before Roy could restrain him, his friend was running hunched into the wind, his hands covering his face from the oncoming sand.

Roy stood to run after Walter, but it was too late to follow him. He ducked back down and cursed to himself. He knew that his friend would have to be very lucky to make it out of the storm alive.

Less than a minute later, the dense cloud of sand

enveloped the men. Roy pressed himself to the ground and covered his mouth with his hat in order to breathe. The sand had turned everything around him into a thick grey fog, and when he looked to his sides, he was unable to see the others who were only a few feet away.

The storm blew over them for nearly an hour, and when it finally passed, the sky cleared, instantly revealing the intense Gobi sun. As the men stood up to shake the sand from their clothes, Walter appeared in the distance staggering toward them. His entire body was stained yellow and, with each plodding step, grains of sand shook from his tangled hair.

"Walter! You're all right!" Roy ran to embrace his friend. "Thank God you made it!"

"I almost didn't, Roy." Walter said as he flopped onto the ground. "I saved those fossils, though. I think the Gobi was just trying to make sure we earned everything we took out of it."

The men returned to camp to wash up, and the next day they prepared the fossils for transport. The nights in the Gobi were now turning cold, signaling the end of the brief Mongolian summer. Despite the possibility of locating more fossils, Roy knew that winter was just around the corner. Rather than return to Urga and drive back to Beijing in a possible snowstorm, Roy and the men agreed to seek a quicker way through the Gobi. Then they would meet the camel caravan at the predetermined location and press on to Northern China.

As they loaded the vehicles and drove off across the desert, they were unaware that they would soon lose their way in the vast emptiness of the Gobi. And, when it seemed they faced certain death, they would stumble upon one of the greatest discoveries of dinosaur bones the world had ever seen.

CHAPTER 14

SKELETONS AND BANDITS

AS ROY GAZED AT THE SUN SETTING OVER the Flaming Cliffs, he marveled at how lucky his day had been. He began it lost in the desert, desperate to navigate a shortcut to reach the camel caravan and the road leading back to China. While the morning hours ticked away, and the team seemed no closer to finding their way, Roy started to wonder if they would make it out of the Gobi alive.

After passing through a blinding sandstorm, Roy led the vehicles up a sloping plateau and was thankful to see a lone *ger* in the distance. He immediately stopped, and leaving the men at the cars, walked to the *ger* with

Damdin, the expedition's translator, to ask directions. Just after discovering from the nomads that Merin and the camels were nearby, Roy and Damdin heard a shout. When they came running, they found that Shackelford, who had wandered from the vehicles for only a few minutes, had accidentally discovered a beautiful canyon rich with dinosaur bones—the place Roy and the others dubbed the Flaming Cliffs.

Damdin walked up to Roy and sat cross-legged in the dirt beside him. He fumbled in the folds of his *dell* and, pulling out a short telescope, scanned the cliffs below.

"The old herdsman back at the *ger* told me that this place is called *Shavar Us*," Damdin said to Roy, looking through the telescope. "That means muddy water, so there must be a small lake around here somewhere. He also said that we'd better leave tomorrow if we want to get out of the desert. It's going to start freezing at night."

"No worries, old friend. We'll be well on our way at dawn. We should be back at headquarters by the end of the week."

The team set off early the next morning, and after a

hard day's drive, they pulled into the small oasis of *Sair Us* where they found Merin watering the camels. He jogged to the cars in his heavy pointed-toe boots and embraced the men.

"I thought the desert had swallowed you!" he laughed, whipping his long braided ponytail over his shoulder. "Even the camels were worried!"

"Well, we barely made it out," Roy said, "For a while there, I thought we were goners."

Supply caravan at the Flaming Cliffs.

The men celebrated their reunion by opening Roy's last bottle of bourbon, which they dug out of Merin's saddlebag and used to toast the success of the first expedition. The next day, after discussing the road conditions back to Kalgan with Merin, the men started loading the vehicles with enough food and water for the journey out of the desert. They packed the dinosaur bones and skins into crates and tied them to the sides of the camels. As soon as the men finished, Merin bid them farewell, agreeing to return the camels to the expedition's stable in Kalgan two weeks later. The team got back in the vehicles and started driving south, hoping to arrive in Beijing before the first snowfall of the season.

Once they arrived back at headquarters, Roy wired a report of their success back to the museum. In only their first summer, they had discovered hundreds of complete and partial dinosaur skeletons as well as insect and plant fossils from the late Cretaceous period. The team had also mapped nearly a thousand miles of uncharted territory and had retrieved more mammal specimens and skins than had ever been collected in Central Asia. The news of the expedition's discoveries spread rapidly throughout America, and Roy soon became one of the country's most talked about celebrities.

Rather than return to New York and enjoy his growing fame, Roy decided to remain in Beijing and plan the next summer's expedition. He spent much of the year preparing for the trip by purchasing new vehicles and camels, carefully planning their route through the Gobi, and recruiting new scientists to join the expedition. Roy also struggled to replace Bayard Colgate, who had to return to America to manage his father's toothpaste and soap empire. Since the expedition relied heavily on such a new invention as the automobile, the chief mechanic was of critical importance. After searching for weeks, Roy found just the person he needed.

Mac Young was a tough, barrel-chested Marine who had worked as a guard and repairman at the American Embassy compound in Beijing for the previous two years. As soon as Roy met Mac and learned of his courageous adventures around the world and his skills at fixing vehicles, he hired him on the spot. The two men became fast friends, and for the next several months, Mac was Roy's right-hand man. While Roy planned the details of the expedition from headquarters, Mac drove on dozens of trips through bandit-infested territory transporting supplies from Beijing to Kalgan and onward to the Mongolian frontier.

With the onset of spring, the scientists and staff from America began arriving at headquarters. When the last of the plans had been finalized and all of the equipment and provisions secured, the Central Asian Expeditions were once again underway. The team left Kalgan in their caravan of six shiny new Dodge Roadsters. They stopped at various places in Northern China and on the out-skirts of the Gobi to excavate potential sites for dinosaur bones. Merin had set off with the camels two weeks earlier intending to rendezvous with the vehicles at the Flaming Cliffs.

A few days before reaching the Flaming Cliffs, Roy decided to return to Kalgan to pick up extra supplies and see if any telegrams had arrived from Osborn. Mac drove with him in a separate car and after speeding across the desert for two days, they approached the pass leading to the Chinese border.

The pass was sandwiched between two steep rocky hills, and Mac followed closely behind Roy as they slowly ascended to the summit. When they reached the top, they dipped down into the narrow valley and maneuvered carefully between the hills. Halfway down the pass, just as the road cleared and they began to pick up speed, Roy screeched to a sudden stop.

Mac slammed on the brakes and skidded down the hill. When the dust cleared, Mac saw that he had come within inches of slamming into Roy's rear bumper.

"You all right, Roy?" he said, turning off the engine and leaning out the window. He saw Roy sitting completely still and wondered if his friend had been injured.

Mac got out of his car to check on Roy. He closed the dust-stained steel door and began walking down the hill when he froze. A half-mile below at the bottom of the pass were four bandits on horseback. Each man wore a thin dust-covered *dell* and had a long musket slung across his back. While Mac stood still, one of the bandits eased his horse a few steps forward and drew his musket, aiming it at the vehicles.

Roy whispered over his shoulder while keeping his eyes on the bandits. "Just get back behind the wheel, Mac. Nice and slow."

Mac nodded and eased himself back into the driver's seat of the convertible.

"We've got only one way out of this," Roy said still looking straight ahead. "I want you to stay here and cover me."

"We're turning back up the valley?"

"We'd never get out, Mac. It's too steep to turn, and besides, those bandits have got the draw on us. Even if they missed, they'd be on us in less than a minute."

"Then, that means . . . wait a minute, Roy. You're not actually going to . . ."

"Right, Mac. I'm going to charge them. I'm betting that the car will spook those horses. It's our only way out, and you know it. Just stay here and give me cover fire if I need it."

Roy slipped the car into drive while keeping his foot

on the brake. He tightened his hat over his brow to block the sun reflecting off the windshield and looked down the pass at the bandits taking aim at his car. He then slowly unholstered his revolver and steadied the gun in his left hand, balancing it on the edge of the car door. With his right hand, he gripped the steering wheel and, after signaling Mac, he slammed his foot on the gas pedal.

The car rocketed down the pass, and Roy fired off three quick shots, which landed at the horses' hooves. The bandits attempted to shoot back, but as soon as their horses heard the roar of the car engine, they bucked wildly, throwing two of the riders to the ground. The other two men dropped their muskets as they frantically grabbed the reins, fighting to stay in the saddle. The sound of the approaching car grew louder, and as it echoed through the pass, the horses grew even more frenzied. Roy fired another shot into the air, and the horses wheeled around, flinging the remaining bandits against the side of the hill. The four empty-saddled horses then galloped off across the desert.

Roy skidded to a stop in front of the bandits and quickly reloaded. He stood up in the car and covered the men with his pistol. He watched as the bandits rolled in the dirt and slowly raised themselves to their knees. As soon as they saw Roy, they lifted their hands in the air and closed their eyes thinking they would be killed.

Instead, Roy commanded them to leave. *"Yav! Yav!"* he ordered. When the bandits refused to budge, he raised his gun high into the air and squeezed the trigger. "I said, *'Yav!'* Go! Get out of here!" The bandits then jumped to their feet with their arms still in the air. Roy fired off another shot, and when they turned to run, one of the men slipped on the untied sash of his *dell* and collided with the three others, knocking them to the ground like bowling pins. Roy burst out laughing as he saw the men who had tried to kill him only minutes earlier now lying on the ground in a tangled heap.

The bandits quickly jumped to their feet again and hobbled bow-legged after their horses. The man who had slipped left his sash in the dirt and took off after the others. Roy chuckled to himself as he watched the lone bandit stagger across the plain, tripping occasionally over the folds of his *dell* and falling face first into the dirt.

Roy and Mac drove on to Kalgan and met up with the rest of the team back at the Flaming Cliffs. The towering buttes and sharp canyons were just as they remembered, and the white-flagged stakes marking the locations of dinosaur skeletons and fossils were still intact from the year before. After hastily setting up camp, the men threw themselves into excavating the area.

The first of their many discoveries at the Flaming Cliffs was a small dinosaur with a bird-like horned head and a large rounded plate at the top of its skull. After analyzing its location in the rock and the other fossils found nearby, Granger and the other scientists determined that the seven-foot-long dinosaur lived during the Cretaceous period and was a herbivore, or plant-eater. In honor of the leader of the expedition, the scientists named the dinosaur *Protoceratops andrewsi*— First Horned Face Andrews.

After finding dozens of other dinosaur bones and prehistoric fossils over the next several days, the team

Protoceratops andrewsi. *This dinosaur was named andrewsi after Roy Chapman Andrews. The first part of the name means "first horned face."*

Velociraptor *or Quick Robber. This is the dinosaur that was featured in the book and movie,* Jurassic Park.

found another unknown skeleton buried in the sand. They took several days painstakingly removing it from the ground and were astonished by the dinosaur's similar skeletal structure to modern day birds. It had a long snout, stiff tail, and two powerful legs with sharp claws and teeth that were clearly used to attack and consume prey. They named it *Velociraptor*—Quick Robber.

For the rest of the month, the Flaming Cliffs continued to provide the most pristine dinosaur specimens the scientists had ever come across. The men were now spending almost sixteen hours a day excavating the canyons and examining the astonishing variety of specimens. But, the most spectacular discovery was yet to come. While digging by himself, George Olsen, a scientist new to the expedition, happened upon something that seemed strangely out of place. Upon closer inspection, however, it would come to be one of the most astounding breakthroughs in the history of paleontology.

CHAPTER 15

AN AMAZING DISCOVERY

WHILE ROY AND THE OTHER SCIENTISTS were relaxing in camp recounting the day's work, the usually quiet Olsen brought up a discovery he had made earlier in the day. It seemed illogical, but something in the back of his mind refused to let it drop.

"I was excavating in the rock on the other side of the cliffs," he began, the other scientists around the table turning toward him, "and after picking away the outer layer of dirt on a small ledge, I found some eggshells."

"Eggshells?" Granger said, "How could that be? This entire area is Cretaceous. As you well know, Olsen, birds didn't emerge until much later. They must have fallen there accidentally . . ."

"That's just it," Olsen said, interrupting Granger. "There shouldn't be eggs there at all, but there are. I don't know what to make of it."

Roy stood up and looked around the table. "I think we'd better take a look at those eggs," he said. "Who knows? They might have been left by a new species of bird." Roy put his hat on and began walking down the cliffs. Olsen and the others slid their chairs in, grabbed their rock picks, and followed Roy into the canyon.

Olsen caught up with Roy and led the men to the site. Arranged in a semi-circle were three slightly chipped oval eggs about six inches long. They lay only feet from where several *Protoceratops* skeletons had been discovered the day before. The men stood back, allowing Olsen and Granger to kneel and inspect the nest.

"Do you think they might be dinosaur eggs?" Roy asked, voicing the question on everyone's mind.

Olsen was deep in concentration and looked up squinting into the sun more than a minute later.

"Well, Roy, we don't really know what to make of it. We've got to be skeptical. If these are dinosaur eggs, it'll be the news of the century."

Olsen went back to the eggs, leaving Roy and the others to peer down over his shoulder. As Roy watched Olsen use a dentist's pick to delicately fleck away the dirt that encrusted the shells, he knew how important these eggs might be. Up until that moment, no scientist had ever concluded whether dinosaurs gave birth to live off-spring, like mammals, or hatched eggs like reptiles. Fifty

George Olsen and Andrews at a nest of dinosaur eggs.

years earlier, an egg of the same size had been located at a dig in Europe, but it hadn't been proven to be laid by a dinosaur.

"Wait! I think we've got something!" Olsen said, his voice shaking with excitement. He took out the magnifying glass from his back pocket and held it over a small hole in one of the eggs.

"My God!" he exclaimed, dropping the magnifying glass out of his hand into the dirt. He looked up at the faces hovering above him.

"Gentlemen, we now have conclusive proof that dinosaurs laid eggs. Have a peek inside."

Olsen stood up and passed the magnifying glass to Granger. When it was Roy's turn to look, he knelt in the sand and peered into the shell more than sixty-five million years old. Inside, he saw an amazingly well-preserved embryo of what was unquestionably a baby dinosaur.

The men spent the rest of the day digging at the site and found several more egg nests. Olsen and Granger also dug in the rock directly above the first nest, and just under the surface, they discovered another unknown dinosaur. Like the *velociraptor,* it had a bird-like appearance and powerful jaws. As the skeleton was almost lying on top of the nest and its arm seemed to be poised in a clawing motion, it appeared that the dinosaur was attempting to eat the eggs when it was likely buried by a sudden sandstorm. When the skeleton was eventually returned to the museum in New York, other scientists confirmed this idea and named it *Oviraptor*— Egg Robber.

With the discovery of the dinosaur eggs at the Flaming Cliffs, Roy became an even bigger celebrity than before. When he returned to America that autumn, he was the most sought-after public speaker in the country and was interviewed by journalists from around the world. Dozens of parties were held in his honor and he dined with movie stars, politicians, and famous scientists. Despite the many distractions of his growing fame, Roy continued to work vigorously for the Central Asian Expeditions. He spent months traveling the country lecturing and raising funds, and finally in mid-1924 he was ready to return to headquarters in Beijing and begin preparing for the latest journey to the Gobi.

The expedition of 1925 proved to be the largest yet. Roy found several new paleontologists, geologists, and botanists to join the scientific team and hired almost two dozen new assistants, porters, and cooks. He also purchased new vehicles and over a hundred camels.

When Roy was finished planning, he traveled to the capital of Mongolia to arrange permission for the expedition to work in the country. Roy had not been to Urga in two years, and in that short period of time, he found the city transformed. The vibrant streets once brimming with merchants, lamas, and herdsmen had turned deathly quiet. Somber-looking police in grey wool uniforms patrolled the sidewalks, stopping and questioning passersby.

When Roy had last visited in 1923, Mongolia was still recovering from a violent revolution where thousands of people were killed. After several major battles, the Mongolian communists, backed by the Russian army, emerged victorious.

After forming their new government, however, the communists began enforcing a strict system of controlling all of the country's property, businesses, and animal herds. In order to ensure that the population followed their orders, communist officials closely monitored the capital with a network of police and spies. As their power rapidly grew, the government also sought to banish the influence of foreigners, like Roy and his expedition, who they believed threatened their tight control of Mongolia.

Roy spent weeks in Ulaanbaatar, the capital's new name, negotiating with the government to allow the expedition to proceed. The officials wouldn't budge, and Roy grew frustrated. After getting nowhere and being followed wherever he went, Roy was ready to cancel the expedition.

At the last moment, one of his Mongolian friends who had close ties to the communists intervened and brokered a deal. Amazingly, the expedition would be permitted to return to the Gobi on the condition that all discoveries would be shared equally with the government. Roy hastily agreed, and drove back to Beijing the next day. Less than a month later, the Central Asian Expedition departed once again for the desert with Roy and Mac leading the way in their new Dodge convertibles.

Throughout the summer, the team found dinosaur bones and fossils in several locations in the Gobi. They visited the Flaming Cliffs one last time to excavate the skeletons they were unable to remove two years earlier. The scientists spent almost two weeks unearthing *Protoceratops* and *Oviraptor* bones as well as locating other egg nests that dotted the hillside. While searching through one of the smaller canyons that they hadn't visited since 1922, the Flaming Cliffs offered yet one more tantalizing discovery.

One late afternoon, Roy wandered beneath the sharply descending hills with Granger and two other scientists. While they scanned the rocks looking for signs of dinosaur bones, Granger nearly tripped over a long, flat rock sticking out of the hillside. He looked down and noticed something that he never imagined he would see in the middle of the Gobi. Scattered over the rock and the nearby sand were dozens of small arrowheads, fragments of rough pottery, and round scraping instruments. Granger called to the others and ducked to the ground to investigate.

"What have you got, Walter?" Roy asked, kneeling beside him in the sand.

Walter picked up several pieces, showing them to Roy and the other scientists. "The wind must have blown the dirt off the rock and exposed all of these. We'll find out exactly how old they are back at the museum, but they look to be late Paleolithic. I'd say ten to twenty thousand years old. Of course, back then this was no desert. It was open grassland with rivers everywhere. I'll bet the people who fashioned these tools roamed all over and had plenty of wildlife to hunt."

"Osborn will be thrilled to get these," Roy said as he marveled at the craftsmanship of a large arrowhead. "Let's get the others down here and scour the area. We've only got a few days left before we need to head home."

Before they left the Flaming Cliffs, the team located hundreds of other Paleolithic tools and artifacts. In the same canyon, several extremely rare mammal and reptile skeletons were also discovered. When Roy and the others surveyed all of the specimens they had obtained, they knew that this summer's expedition was even more successful than the one two years earlier.

They left the Flaming Cliffs and drove southeast toward China. At their last camp in the Gobi, about fifty miles from the border, the weather began to turn cold. The temperature at night dipped to almost below freezing, and the men slept in their cots bundled under sheepskin blankets. The night before they were set to leave, Roy was nodding off when he heard screaming coming from one of the tents. He jumped out of bed in

Oviraptor *or Egg Thief*
Andrews and Olsen believed that this dinosaur, found above some dinosaur eggs,
was stealing eggs from a nest. Seventy years later, it was discovered that the
oviraptor *was not stealing eggs but had laid the eggs and was incubating them.*

long johns and bare feet and ran outside joining the other men racing for the tent.

Roy pulled back the flap and saw Granger and Norman Lovell, Mac's assistant mechanic, kneeling on their cots scanning the ground frantically. Roy peered into the tent, and in the sliver of moonlight leaking through the opening, he saw two four-foot long vipers slither out from under Walter's bed and burrow under a crate at the back of the tent.

"Are they gone, Roy?" Walter nervously asked. "Gimme your gun just in case!"

"Relax, my friend," Roy said. "They've probably just come in to get out of the cold. I doubt they'll bite."

"Easy enough for you to say standing out there!" Norman said as he eased out of bed. Just as he was about to put his foot down, Roy saw another slithering tail reflected in the moonlight.

"Don't move, Norman! You may want to have a look under your bed."

Norman shined the flashlight at the ground and saw a sleeping viper coiled around the wooden legs of his cot.

He jerked back in fright and turned to the others looking through the flap of his tent.

"Guys, will you kindly *get us outta here!*"

"Okay, okay," Roy said. "We'll be right back. Just sit tight."

The men ran back to their tents and scrounged for implements to kill the snakes. Roy grabbed a large shovel from under his cot and sat down to put his shoes on. As he lifted one of his boots over his numb foot, another viper fell out, slapping against his leg and thudding to the ground. He jumped back, and after catching his breath, lifted the shovel and swung it down, killing the snake instantly.

After disposing of the snakes in Norman and Walter's tent, the men searched throughout the camp killing nearly two dozen more. When they arrived at the dining tent, Walter entered first carrying a large iron rock pick in both hands. He crept silently past the mess table and saw a long fat snake lying underneath one of the benches.

"I've got you now!" he said and raised the pick high above his head, skewering the body into the ground. Roy clicked on his flashlight, shined it at the snake, and burst out laughing.

"Well done, Walter. You've killed one of Mac's engine pipes!"

"Oh, shut it, Roy." Walter said. At that moment, Roy stepped back toward the door, and his foot landed on something soft and round. He let out a howl and pounded the ground with his shovel before jumping onto the table. This time, it was Walter's turn to laugh. He turned on the gas lantern hanging from the roof and announced with a comedic air: "Ladies and Gentlemen, the famed desert explorer and daring adventurer Roy Chapman Andrews has slain the elusive coiled rope of the Gobi!"

"Funny, Walter. Real funny."

Rather than sleeping on their cots and looking out for more snakes, the two friends walked back to the tents and gathered their blankets. On the hood of Roy's car, they spent their last night in the Gobi, reminiscing about their adventures and gazing at the stars in the cloudless desert sky.

EPILOGUE

"HERE WE ARE, SIR. THE ADDRESS YOU REQUESTED."

"I'll be just a minute," Roy said, speaking in rusty Chinese to the driver.

"Take as long as you want, sir. I'll wait right here."

Roy stepped out of the car into the humid Beijing morning. Though it had been more than three years since he was last in the city, it seemed that not a moment had passed. He stood on the corner taking in the everyday street life that he remembered so well. Just opposite the road, a young girl in pigtails handed a street vendor a wrinkled note and skipped away from his cart with a stick of candied crabapples. Pigeons pecked at scraps of garbage and watermelon rinds and fluttered away with the passing of bicycles. Shops were just opening for business, and Roy watched as a portly woman in slippers and an apron carefully arranged a pyramid of square metal tea boxes in her window display. Roy was pleased that little had changed on this street since he first set foot on it more than a decade ago.

He closed the car door and turned the corner into a narrow lane shaded by high brick walls. He walked slowly, passing a small clutch of old men sitting on rickety chairs smoking thin, long-stemmed pipes and playing dominoes. Halfway down the street, he came to a large iron-barred gate. He stopped, took off his hat, and stood for a moment, gazing into what had been the former headquarters of the Central Asian Expeditions.

Roy took out a long skeleton key from the pocket of his sport coat and gently inserted it in the lock. The gate creaked open, and Roy stepped into the courtyard. The main garden, which had once been luxuriantly tended with flowers and pools of goldfish, was now a tangle of overgrown grass and weeds. The sloping roofed buildings were also in a state of disrepair. The paint was peeling away on the walls and the fine wooden latticework that covered the windows was becoming misshapen by years of exposure in the harsh Beijing weather.

The silence of the courtyard was broken only by Roy's footsteps echoing off the cobblestones as he strolled toward the main building. He passed the garage, horse stables, and servants' quarters, all empty now, and walked up the short flight of stairs to what was once the expedition's meeting hall. He slid back the dull-red wooden door and stepped inside.

The room was bare save for the dust floating in the beams of sunlight streaming in through the two large bay windows. Roy had first entered this spacious hall in 1920, almost fifteen years ago. What was now considered the century's most daring and successful scientific expedition had been planned almost entirely in this room, and while he stood quietly and closed his eyes, Roy could picture those bygone days once more.

The expedition of 1925 had been a phenomenal success, and as soon as Roy and his team returned to headquarters in Beijing, they began planning a return voyage. However, after almost two years of delicate negotiations with the communist government of Mongolia and the Chinese warlords that controlled all passage through Kalgan, Roy was unable to obtain permission to explore the Gobi. The team therefore settled for two expeditions in 1928 and 1930 to the southern section of the Gobi located in Inner Mongolia, China.

Although the discoveries made on these two trips were not as sensational as those at the Flaming Cliffs, many rare specimens of dinosaurs and prehistoric mammals were recovered and eventually placed in the display galleries at the museum. Roy intended to return to the desert again in 1932, but after the Japanese empire seized Northern China, this became impossible. When he realized that another Central Asian Expedition was no longer viable, he returned to New York, where he divided his time between working at the museum, writing an account of his adventures, lecturing, and traveling.

When Henry Fairfield Osborn retired, Roy was promoted to vice-director of the museum, and when the director suddenly died only a few months later, Roy was appointed to lead the institution. After less than a year on the job, Osborn passed away as well. Roy was crushed by the death of his mentor and best friend, and to relieve his depression and the strain of directing the museum, he decided to take a brief vacation. He returned to Beijing to rest and enjoy a few weeks in his favorite city. Most of all, though, he looked forward to seeing his old home in the heart of the capital.

Roy opened his eyes and looked again through the dusty, empty room. He remembered how the great meeting hall had once looked—the leather couches arranged next to the fireplace, the walls covered with stacks of books and Chinese paintings, the grand piano in the corner, and the large oak table in the center of the room covered with maps, fossils, and photographs of Mongolia. It was all packed away now, but Roy could still imagine the years he had spent in this very room planning the five Central Asian Expeditions.

Even though the original idea that had sparked the expeditions was never proven (Osborn's theory that prehistoric mammals and humans had originated in Central Asia), Roy and his team astounded the world with some of the most significant scientific discoveries ever made. He knew, though, that after all the hard work and dedication he put into the expeditions, luck had also played a major part in its success.

Roy drifted to the window and gazed out at the courtyard. As he looked at the overgrown garden he remembered how lucky he had been throughout his entire life. He thought of how he and his team had narrowly escaped death in the Gobi and discovered the Flaming Cliffs by chance only hours later. He recalled other times from earlier in his career, like his narrow escapes from bandits and the time Mirando warned him at the last second of the deadly python waiting to pounce on him. Roy also recalled the traumatic incident from his youth when he barely managed to survive after his dear friend Monty had drowned in that cold Wisconsin river.

After looking out the window for another minute, Roy turned to leave. He had enjoyed reliving some of his old memories from his days as an explorer, but he had never been one to dwell in the past. He chose not to rest on his accomplishments and always looked to the horizon, planning his next expedition. Besides, this was only a short vacation. He had a museum to run.

As he walked away from the window, his hand brushed against the sill, spilling a thin film of sand onto the floor. He remembered that sandstorms often blew in from Mongolia during the spring, blanketing the capital. Holding his hand up to the sunlight, he examined the remnants of the desert that had revealed to him so many of its ancient secrets. Roy Chapman Andrews grinned and rubbed the fine grains of Gobi sand through his fingertips for the last time.

BIBLIOGRAPHY

I have based my book on conversations with Mongolians who knew of Andrews and his adventures, as well as the books listed below, many of which he wrote himself.

Books by Roy Chapman Andrews:

Camps and Trails in China. New York: Appleton (1918).

Across Mongolian Plains. New York: Appleton (1921).

This Business of Exploring. New York: G. Putnam and Sons (1935).

Under a Lucky Star: A Lifetime of Adventure. New York: Viking (1943).

Books by Others:

Dragon Hunter by Charles Gallenkamp. New York: Viking (2001).

Dinosaurs of the Flaming Cliffs by Michael Novacek. New York: Doubleday (1996).

INDEX

Note: Page numbers in *italics* refer to maps and illustrations.

181

ABOUT THE AUTHOR

Author Roger Cohen first learned of Roy Chapman Andrews as a Peace Corps volunteer in Southwestern Mongolia. He also worked in the Mongolian capital of Ulaanbaatar and has traveled extensively throughout the country. An English instructor by profession, Roger is also comfortable riding camels and speaking Mongolian to desert nomads. He currently lives in San Antonio, Texas with his wife. This is his first book.